Saving Open Space

Saving Open Space

The Politics of
Local Preservation in California

Daniel Press

UNIVERSITY OF CALIFORNIA PRESS
Berkeley · Los Angeles · London

University of California Press
Berkeley and Los Angeles, California

University of California Press, Ltd.
London, England

© 2002 by the Regents of the University of California

Library of Congress Cataloging-in-Publication Data

Press, Daniel, 1962–.
   Saving open space : the politics of local preservation
in California / Daniel Press.
      p.   cm.
   Includes bibliographical references and index.
   ISBN 0-520-23387-5 (alk. paper).—
ISBN 0-520-23388-3 (pbk. : alk. paper)
      1. Open spaces—California.   2. Landscape
protection—California.   3. Open spaces—
Government policy—California.   4. Landscape
protection—Government policy—California.
I. Title.

HT393.C2 P74   2002
333.77'16'09794—dc21   2001007756

Manufactured in Canada

13   12   11   10   09   08   07   06   05   04
10   9   8   7   6   5   4   3   2   1

The paper used in this publication meets the minimum
requirements of ANSI/NISO Z39.48–1992 (R 1997)
(*Permanence of Paper*).

To Isobel, and all of California's children

Contents

Illustrations and Tables

TABLES

County Abbreviations

Al	Alameda	Pl	Placer
Am	Amador	Ri	Riverside
Bu	Butte	Sac	Sacramento
Ca	Calaveras	SB	Santa Barbara
CC	Contra Costa	SBen	San Benito
Co	Colusa	SBer	San Bernardino
ED	El Dorado	SCl	Santa Clara
Fr	Fresno	SCr	Santa Cruz
Gl	Glenn	SD	San Diego
Hu	Humboldt	SF	San Francisco
Im	Imperial	Sh	Shasta
Ke	Kern	SJ	San Joaquin
Ki	Kings	SLO	San Luis Obispo
LA	Los Angeles	SM	San Mateo
Las	Lassen	Sol	Solano
Lk	Lake	Son	Sonoma
Mad	Madera	St	Stanislaus
Mar	Marin	Su	Sutter
Men	Mendocino	Te	Tehama
Mer	Merced	Tu	Tulare
Mo	Monterey	Ve	Ventura
Na	Napa	Yo	Yolo
Ne	Nevada	Yu	Yuba
Or	Orange		

Acknowledgments

A good bottle of Zinfandel and a nice dinner got me started on this adventure through California's landscapes and history. Tom Rochon was visiting me on a well-deserved sabbatical from his post at the Claremont Graduate University when I first discussed with him my admiration for local preservation efforts around the state. Tom has an uncanny ability to listen to musings and half-baked observations, find the gem within, and hold it up for his friends and colleagues to view. Robert Putnam's book *Making Democracy Work* had recently been accumulating its accolades; civic culture and the performance of local institutions were in the air. Thanks to Tom (and some very positive mail from Putnam), I found both encouragement and conceptual models for the story of local preservation in California.

Dan Mazmanian is another perennial supporter. You haven't lived until you've spent a July afternoon discussing ideas with him outside his cabin at Silver Lake in the eastern Sierra. I've had that good fortune for most of the life of this project, and his remarks have always taken me a step further.

As I floated my ideas, early observations, and research designs, I received excellent comments from colleagues in my home Department of Environmental Studies, at the University of California, Santa Cruz. These include Jenny Anderson, Dan Doak, Margaret FitzSimmons, Steve Gliessman, David Goodman, Brent Haddad, Rich Howarth, Julie Lockwood, Marc Mangel, Steve Minta, Roberto Sanchez, and Michael Soulé.

No one told me that my data-collection ambitions were likely to triple the length of time it would take to complete the project; fortunately, I was generously supported by the U.S. Environmental Protection Agency (grant number R825226), the John Randolph Haynes and Dora Haynes Foundation of Los Angeles, and the Social Sciences Division at UC Santa Cruz. Clyde Bishop, from the EPA, has been a steadfast supporter. These funding sources permitted me to implement a full-employment policy for what seemed like a generation of graduate and undergraduate researchers. Among the graduate assistants I thank are Alan Balch, Cathy Fogel, Betsy Herbert, Karsten Mueller, Jonathan Scheuer, and Paul Steinberg. Each of them cheerfully took on the most tedious data collection and entry tasks but also brought to bear shrewd insights, intelligence, and moral support for multiple research seasons. No advisor could ask for a better graduate cohort. Other assistants and undergraduate victims include Caroline Berger, Karin Foster, Rosalie Hackett, Crystal Hernandez, Peter Lemoine, Clodagh Meade, Jen McGraw, Michelle Renée, and Rachel Warner. Early in the project, Addy Chuleff ran a very successful focus group in Ventura County; I am grateful to her and the group members for their time and insights.

Over the years, I had generous technical assistance for mapping and statistical analyses from John Deck, Marc Los Huertos, and Hope Malcom. Each of them bailed me out of technical pickles without so much as a furrowed brow. The Fates smiled upon me again when they sent me Henrietta Brown and Judith Burton, whose painstaking transcriptions of taped interviews ensured that I could actually listen to my respondents as they spoke, instead of writing frantically throughout.

Some institutions are blessed with a miraculous staff: for the last three decades the Environmental Studies Department at the University of California, Santa Cruz, has flourished in no small part thanks to Jenny Anderson, Linda Armstrong, Juanita Nama, and Andrea Welles.

For my phone survey I was marvelously assisted by Rufus Browning and Terra Scherr of the Policy Research Institute at San Francisco State University. Rufus and Terra, along with their crew of callers, permitted me to successfully craft and implement a survey instrument that I could never have executed on my own. Many of my other data had been collected by state agencies; discovering and retrieving these fell to UCSC's government publications librarians, who did so patiently, expertly, and cheerfully. They include Jan Becking, Cynthia Jahns, and Joanne Nelson; indeed, our librarians consistently show me just how good a library can be for a school's faculty.

I am grateful to all my interview respondents, and I would like to thank especially Esther Feldman, Madelyn Glickfeld, Eric Jessen, Gerry Meral, Ron Miska, Gary Patton, Mike Rotkin, and Audrey Rust. Denzil Verardo of the California Department of Parks and Recreation—as fine a historian of the state as they come—was generous with data, insights, and enthusiasm. The staff at the State Board of Equalization was kind, welcoming, and forthright with their data on land use changes in the state.

Chris Klyza read the manuscript for the University of California Press, giving me some of the most constructive advice I have ever seen—he redefined for me the practice and purpose of peer review. I thank Blake Edgar at the Press for championing the manuscript while giving me finely tuned suggestions. I also thank the production staff at the Press, especially Dore Brown, Bonita Hurd, and Nicole Stephenson. Victor Schiffrin has been taking photographs for my projects for a long time now; I am grateful for yet another round. I also had the good fortune of securing Elspeth Pope's talents for producing a meticulous index.

My students in Environmental Studies renew me with their energy and engagement; they have often been my first audience, appreciative, bright, skeptical, and good-humored. My family and friends have been graciously enthusiastic throughout. I thank them all, and especially Esther Press-McManus, Richard Press, Talya Press, Isobel Press, Julian Dahan, Alison Russell, Charlie McManus, Michael Potepan, Donna Ficarotta, Michael Lippitz, Dean Clark, and Sarah Wiener-Boone.

CHAPTER I

Introduction

What could be done to stop the destruction of the country-
side? By the end of the 1950s, the question was at the heart
of a new kind of conservation effort. . . . In a number of
ways, the effort to preserve open space was a critical stage
in the evolution of the modern environmental movement.

Adam Rome, "William Whyte, Open Space,
and Environmental Activism," 1998

This book is about land preservation against the odds. Despite their reputation as effective obstructionists, environmentalists lose far more frequently than they win, especially when it comes to land use conflicts.
Moreover, the rewards for local policy entrepreneurs to pursue pro-
growth policies are usually far greater than they are for pushing slow
growth, antigrowth, or preservation (Fulton 1997; Schneider et al.
1995). In this book I am concerned with successful preservation in California. Powerful social, economic, and political forces virtually ensure
that proposed developments proceed; however, in some parts of the
country such projects are routinely scaled down or the lands in question
are acquired outright largely because of local slow-growth or land
preservation efforts.

Given the momentum and imperative of growth, one might not expect
much preservation at all. As in other rapidly growing regions of the
United States, land development in California far outstrips preservation
and will continue to do so for years to come. It is all the more remark-
able, then, when local governments and residents manage to set aside
important parcels. But why do some communities preserve more open
space than others? More specifically, what are the conditions for creating
innovative, effective land preservation institutions at the local level?

CALIFORNIA AS OBJECT LESSON

While I address these questions as they play out in a single state, California's responses to the challenges of land conversion and runaway development are not at all unique. News articles featuring the drawbacks of rapid development throughout the country proliferated in the 1990s (Egan 1996, 1998; Kasler 1998; Nivola 1999; Wilson 1999). Many of these cited a familiar mix of bewilderment, frustration, and anger on the part of local residents and their elected officials around the country. In 1998, Vice President Al Gore, already preparing his presidential campaign, concluded that urban sprawl and the attendant loss of habitat, farmland, and recreation areas resonated with voters all over the country (Borenstein and Rogers 1999; Janofsky 1999).

The 1998 general election campaigns staged hundreds of pitched battles, as local politicians and activists used ballot measures to reign in development or pay for land preservation. In a widely cited study that she conducted for the Brookings Institution, Phyllis Myers found no fewer than "240 state and local measures related to conservation, parklands, and smarter growth" appearing on ballots in November 1998. Voters overwhelmingly supported these measures—72 percent received majority approval—often by margins greater than 65 percent (Myers 1999). In the West and Southeast and on the Pacific Coast, ballot measures served as the policy tools of choice. Bond and other finance measures around the country raised at least $4.5 billion, mostly for land acquisition; many other measures imposed urban growth boundaries constraining the areas in which new development would be permitted.

The explosion of land preservation ballot measures showed no signs of abating in either the 1999 off-year election or the November 2000 general election. In 1999, voters passed 92 measures for open space in 22 states (a 90 percent approval rate), raising over $1.8 billion. In November of 2000, voters approved 208 measures in 29 states (an 84 percent approval rate), raising over $7.4 billion (Land Trust Alliance 2001). In many of these states, several jurisdictions considered land preservation funding measures in the same election. Like California cities, counties, and special districts (single-purpose agencies with broad authority), local jurisdictions around the country varied greatly in the approval rates they received for their open space referenda and initiatives—some cities in New Jersey, for example differed by over 40 percent in their approval of very similar open space tax measures *in the same elections* in November of 1998 and 1999 (ibid.). Voters in every state heard the message about sprawl, but not every community listened. These several hundred ballot measures represent a massive political mobilization effort. Bond measures and growth-restricting initiatives are not easy to place on statewide ballots; it is even harder to secure a super-majority of voter support (that is, two-thirds or more of votes cast). That so many measures were on ballots and passed is indicative of voters' pervasive frustration with state and local land use patterns.

In addition to statewide bond financing, "nearly half the states have initiated efforts to influence control, or manage growth," according to a study by Marshall Kaplan and his colleagues. "They involve a collage of different kinds of regulatory initiatives and incentives" (Kaplan et al. 1999, p. 4). Three states—Minnesota, Oregon, and Florida—stand out as particularly active in slowing growth.

The Minnesota legislature enacted region-based tax sharing in the 1960s as part of an evolving set of institutions that would eventually result in the Twin Cities Metropolitan Council becoming the "most powerful regional government in the United States" (ibid., p. 5). While legislative coalitions have empowered inner city communities possessing lower fiscal capacities, not even this strong regional approach has prevented sprawl.

In Oregon, growth management efforts for the city of Portland were initiated in 1973 by the governor; the legislature assisted by enacting "a law creating a statewide land-use framework that required urban growth boundaries and consistency among local, regional and state plans. The law encouraged multi-modal transportation initiatives and mandated coordinated transportation and land-use planning" (ibid., p. 6). The three-county Portland metropolitan area elected a regional governing body—the Metropolitan Service District—in 1978, which then established urban growth boundaries around twenty-four cities in the region. This effort to control sprawl has worked, resulting in protection of key forest and agricultural lands and a booming central city, but housing affordability, social welfare, and congestion are still problems. Kaplan and his colleagues doubt that this scenario could be easily replicated in other parts of the country, because Portland is blessed with "a civic culture that places a great premium on the environment" and "a population that generally favors state and regional government intervention in local matters, particularly with respect to growth" (ibid.).

Florida responded to rapid population growth with state legislation imposing "comprehensive planning requirements" on cities and counties, requiring project review and approval for developments with regional impact, and providing "state oversight of lands in which a 'critical state interest' could be demonstrated" (ibid., p. 7). To acquire open space and protect fragile lands, Florida dedicated funds from a real estate transfer tax. However, cities and counties responded with plans that allow for three to five times as much growth as predicted, thereby negating some of the effects of the growth management plans and protecting their own revenues with future increases in sales and property taxes.

In 1985, Florida required local governments to demonstrate concurrency—that is, show that public infrastructure is available before approving further developments. While this law infuriated developers before it was passed, they soon found that they could build relatively easily in areas that had road capacity. In this way, concurrency may have actually fostered sprawl (ibid., p. 8).

Florida also relies on information-sharing and collaboration to foster growth control. Eastward Ho! is a state-initiated effort to redirect growth to areas away from Everglades National Park. The program provides "convincing data concerning the benefits and costs of alternatives" to a collaborative partnership of government, business, and community leaders (ibid., p. 9). While it is too soon to judge the effectiveness of the approach, critics say that more powerful initiatives will likely be needed.

In one of Shutkin's case studies, which took place in New Jersey, the postwar period represents a transition from "a largely rural landscape of farms, villages and towns into a massive suburb" (Shutkin 2000). With almost two-thirds of the state's 4.8 million acres developed, and only 30,000 acres protected as critical habitat, in 1998 New Jersey voters passed not only a $1 billion plan to save vanishing farmland from development but also a constitutional amendment that dedicates up to $98 million annually for open space conservation (ibid., p. 212). Shutkin asked why it took so long for New Jersey residents to act. His answer: suburbanization itself, at least in part. Suburbia "seems to have an insulating and inhibiting effect on individuals' civic will. By being segregated on single lots and forced to depend on automobiles for travel, suburban residents are largely deprived of the opportunity to act collectively and responsively in the face of adverse environmental conditions."

The changes that led to the statewide initiative began at the township and county levels with citizens' efforts. For example, in 1984, citizens of Randolph Township (Morris County) founded a nonprofit named Morris 2000 to actively support protection of open space within the county, as well as promote redevelopment of brownfields (generally, abandoned industrial sites) and the construction of new commuter rail systems. The founders of the group were dedicated to regional solutions that engage citizens. New Jersey became the first state to adopt a bottom-up approach to balance the home rule authority of municipalities with coherent, consistent regional planning (ibid., p. 219). The 1992 State Development and Redevelopment Plan launched a consensus-building process called cross-acceptance, which requires interaction and negotiation at every level of government, the end product being county and municipality master plans that compare favorably with state standards. New Jersey does not have police power over the plans, but it can withhold funding from those that do not comply. In tandem, the nonprofit New Jersey Future started the Sustainable State Project to provide a forum for a wide range of civic and advocacy organizations "to work toward consensus on long-term, measurable quality-of-life goals and to create changes in New Jerseyans' behavior that help achieve those goals" (ibid., p. 222). Barbara Lawrence, the founder of New Jersey Future, stresses that citizens must be involved in the decision-making process, even when this involves technical decisions based on sometimes inscrutable science. The group sponsors leadership conferences to involve citizens in setting goals for sustainability and to find appropriate indicators for measuring their success at reaching those goals.

Despite real differences between California and states like Minnesota, Oregon, Florida, and New Jersey, California's experience with rapid growth and land preservation resembles that of the rest of the nation in four ways. First, the development challenge and the imperative to control sprawl are ubiquitous (Bank of America 1996; Benfield et al. 1999; Sierra Club 1999). Second, local and state governments around the country share a limited set of land preservation and growth management tools (Burby and May 1997). These include direct land acquisition by public or private institutions and various kinds of land use controls, most of which depend on zoning or on leveraging public resources with private payments, gifts, or exactions (Glickfeld et al. 1995). Increasingly, local parks agencies and land trusts around the country also acquire conservation easements on private lands by purchase or gift. Third, the actors involved in development and preservation battles are the same in California as elsewhere—local government, recreation and parks agencies, the U.S. Environmental Protection Agency (EPA), state and federal transportation agencies, private land trusts, the construction industry, and nongovernmental civic organizations (Myers 1999; Wright 1993).

Finally, California mirrors the nation in that its many local communities also vary with respect to their willingness and ability to address over-development by preserving land or instituting growth controls. Like many states, especially those in the Northeast and upper Midwest, California has a strong tradition of home rule and weak state land use controls. This home-rule culture ensures that zoning and land use are the sacred cows of local government; woe betide the state official who tries to take them away. Accordingly, governors and the legislature have consistently shied away from imposing growth controls with real teeth (Pincetl 1999).

California's regions and counties draw on a different mix of institutions and policy tools to accomplish land preservation goals. This regional diversity mirrors the nation's own—witness the importance of land trusts in the Northeast and their near absence in the upper Rocky Mountains, or the very different ways state transportation agencies respond to land use and sprawl. Thus, regions and communities in other states are no more homogeneous in their responses to development and land conversion than are California cities, counties, and regions.

In 1965, Ray Dasmann wrote, "Unless we act now to stop the forces of destruction that are at work, the state that once was green and golden may become an object lesson that shows only what other areas must avoid" (Dasmann, p. 225). What happens in California, the state with the nation's largest population and fastest growth, will be noticed by other states and will also affect them. Moreover, California frequently leads the country in policy innovations, some of which have had a positive effect on environmental resources, such as the 1972 Coastal Act, while others have resulted in governance-crippling antitax measures, such as the 1978 Proposition 13. Finally, not all has been destruction since Dasmann wrote his words of caution: a great deal of land has been preserved and many lessons have been learned along the way. For all the ways in which the Golden State resembles and differs from the rest of the nation, preservation in California communities serves as an object lesson for the rest of the nation, not only in land loss but also in redemption.

THE LAND PRESERVATION PROBLEM IN CALIFORNIA

Open space preservation responds to many of the thorniest land use problems facing growing communities. The litany of development ills is familiar: conversion of productive agricultural lands, loss of rare or endangered species and natural plant and animal communities, impairment of watersheds, and loss of recreation areas. Development patterns and shrinking outdoor recreational areas were already alarming in the mid-1960s, when the state passed a major land conservation bill—the so-called Williamson Act—which gave farmers a tax break in exchange for keeping their land in agriculture. The legislature held numerous special hearings on open space and development (California Legislature 1969). The various reports from the 1960s and 1970s are quite explicit about changes in the landscape; common features of environmentalist pamphlets of the time include maps showing a metropolitan area "with open space" and "without open space" (POS 1969). The ill effect that California's already overheated growth machine was having on habitat and water quality was suspected (see Dasmann 1965) but had not yet been completely documented.

Since the 1970s, a generation of scientists has tracked changes in species composition and habitat quality, watershed conditions, farmland acreage, and outdoor recreational opportunity (Jensen, Torn, and Harte 1993). We now have thirty years of good data on changes in the physical and biological characteristics of the urban fringe—on agricultural and open space land conversions, biodiversity loss, and the health of major watersheds.

Although California gives the impression of vastness in all respects, its landscapes change quickly from valley to valley, forming a mosaic of small places (see figures 1 and 2). Its tumultuous geologic past has bequeathed to California many abruptly changing soil profiles, which harbor small assemblages of rare plant and invertebrate species. Most of these rare species are confined to just one or two of the state's fifty-eight counties; thus there are rare plants and invertebrates in nearly every county (Press et al. 1996).

California's physical, biological, and social landscapes all contribute to an essentially local vulnerability. Habitat types on the urban fringe cannot be protected by setting aside just one or a few big reserves. Even if land at city edges were available and affordable in large parcels, the resulting reserves would be subject to negative "edge effects"—habitat degradation resulting from encroachment by the people, domestic animals, and non-native plants that border protected lands. Moreover, the federal government and state parks system are important partners, but they are not substitutes for preservation close to the urban zone or for greenbelts encircling cities. There are simply too few state and national parks and other recreation areas near growing urban centers—in the Sacramento and San Joaquin Valleys, in the San Francisco Bay Area, and in the South Coast—for the state or federal government to act as the sole recreation and habitat provider.

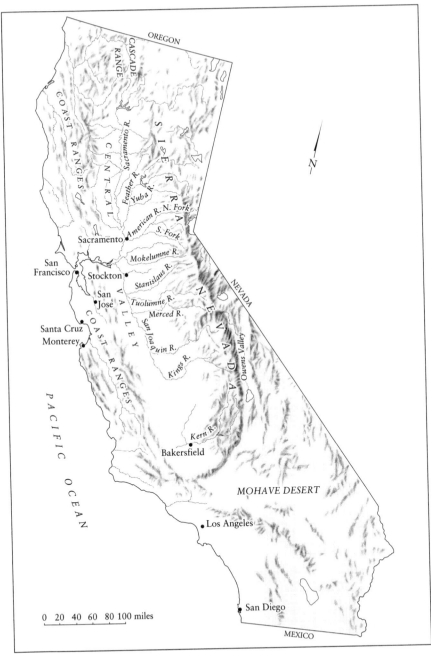

Figure 1. California topography and major rivers.

Figure 2. California counties.

Since 1964, California has lost about a quarter of its farmland, well over 8 million acres, much of it to urban development (US DOA 2000). Very few counties escaped this trend; most lost between 150,000 and 200,000 acres (California Department of Conservation 1984–1998).

Rapid urban growth has its human costs as well. California's population grew from 20 million people in 1970 to 32 million people in 1995, but the number of miles traveled by automobiles in the same period more than doubled. In the 1990s, four of the nation's ten most congested metropolitan areas were in California, prompting even the Republican Wilson administration to conclude that the state could not afford much more growth without serious reinvestment (ARB 1998; US DOT 2001a).[1] The transportation consequences of growth are familiar to anyone commuting long distances from outlying areas with affordable housing to urban centers with highly paid jobs (Wildermuth 1997).

Not surprisingly, air quality has declined in many parts of California. Although Los Angeles experiences far fewer smog alerts today than it did in the 1970s, more of California's urban areas exceed thresholds for healthful air quality. Californians rate air pollution as the state's top environmental problem over every other issue, according to a survey by the Public Policy Institute of California (PPIC) in 2000. In 1980, twenty-eight of fifty-eight counties failed to meet California's own Clean Air Act standards for ozone, one of the most dangerous elements in smog. By the late 1990s, forty counties were out of compliance with these standards (ARB 1998).

THE GROWTH MACHINE

Harvey Molotch depicted local governments as "growth machines," stating that growth is the "political and economic essence of virtually any given locality" (1976, p. 310). Local, politically active elites tend to reach consensus on behalf of population expansion, business growth, infrastructure development, new commerce, and housing construction (Pincetl 1999, p. 256), despite the fact that "growth often costs existing residents more money" than it returns (Molotch 1976, p. 319).

While farmland and species habitats shrank and watersheds declined, the growth machine of the last forty years ensured that cities would grow at astonishing rates. Urban service areas (incorporated areas, or the effective city limits) grew by about 30,000 acres per year during the 1990s. Between 1995 and 2000, California cities increased their urban service areas by about 163,000 acres via annexation (California State Board of

Equalization 1995–2000). Although state and local governments added substantially to their park acreage in this same period, land lost to development or taken out of agricultural production outpaced land preservation by at least 8 acres to 1.

Between 1977 and 1997, California's population grew at a rate of 150,000 to 750,000 people, or 1–3 percent every year (California Department of Finance 1998). Between 1986 and 1997, the real estate–development industry added, on average, 158,000 new housing units annually; the total for this decade was 1.9 million units (ibid., 1999). Powerful political and fiscal incentives from local, state, and federal programs fuel the growth machine in California, and have done so for years (Pincetl 1999, pp. 117, 122, 136). Running on a pro-growth record or platform has for years been a safe, tried and true strategy for success in local politics anywhere in the country. California's semipermanent tax revolt (to paraphrase Peter Schrag) began with Proposition 13, gutting city and county budgets and forcing local government into winner-take-all competitions for strip mall developments that promised big sales-tax revenues. At the same time, the California legislature has steadily siphoned property taxes away from local government, funds that could have been used for building local infrastructure and social programs (Schrag 1998). County supervisors and city council members, once elected, grant developers variances for projects that specifically violate terms of the general plan and chew up farmland and open space while saddling local government with the infrastructure burdens (Fulton 1997; Miller 1998; Pincetl 1999).

The growth machine can go to unusual extremes—including fostering political corruption—where millions of dollars are at stake. In Operation Rezone in Fresno, for example, the FBI pursued a dozen federal indictments leading to several convictions on charges of political-influence peddling. City officials had accepted bribes from developers to rezone lands for development and push through local government infrastructure payments (Arax 1995; Nolte 1999).

By any measure, the development industry outmatches preservationists. An $87 billion industry employing over 560,000 Californians in construction alone (in 1997), development is a force to reckon with (U.S. Census Bureau 2002). Indeed, 1 in 10 Californians was employed in either construction or support industries, including finance, insurance, and real estate, in 1997 (California Department of Finance 1998).

Considering the pervasive and overwhelming clout of development, any land preservation seems extraordinary. In contrast with the lucrative real estate industry, the leadership for open space preservation—which consists of some city or county politicians, small-time environmental activists, and local parks agency officials—has much less influence. There is not much money to be gained in stopping bulldozers even if the landscapes truly are compelling. Nongovernmental organizations working to protect land are typically understaffed, underfunded, and outgunned. Their lawyers often offer their services pro bono, and they are rarely equipped to mount expensive political campaigns in favor of park bonds, other land protection ballot measures, or environment-friendly candidates. The two important exceptions, the David and Lucile Packard Foundation (with its multimillion dollar Conservation Program) and the Trust for Public Land, are statewide or national in scope and fund-raising efforts.

POLICY OUTPUTS AND OUTCOMES

Often at the vanguard of paradoxical trends, California is one of the fastest growing states in the country, but it is also the most ambivalent about change. Despite the political and economic power of the developers, it is not always difficult to drum up anti- or slow-growth rhetoric; in some communities, development is a bad word. Judging by policy outputs—ordinances, legislation, general plan amendments, public pronouncements by local leaders—many communities around California are committed to mitigating, containing, and slowing growth (see Derr 1997). Local frustration with the negative effects of growth is not, however, sufficient for slow-growth or preservation outcomes, thanks in part to California's pervasive ambivalence about development. As Stephanie Pincetl explains so well in her 1999 book on California land use, residents want slower growth as long as they enjoy a strong tax base and rising employment. The PPIC survey conducted in the spring of 2000 demonstrates just how divided public sentiment on growth has become. The survey found that a majority (52 percent) would oppose bond measures allowing local government to acquire land if it meant paying higher property taxes, but large majorities (over 70 percent) want land preservation, especially if paid for by philanthropists or others in the private sector (PPIC 2000). Given this free-rider attitude, it comes as no surprise that local and state leadership remains gridlocked in partisan disputes or unable to resist the fiscal imperatives of growth.

Policy outputs such as local general plans and policy pronouncements reflect a community's best intentions about a problem. However, the realities of implementation often prevent local preservationists from realizing their goals. We must assess on-the-ground outcomes to see whether the extraordinary policy entrepreneurship, local resources, and public expectations that stand behind preservation attempts actually make a difference. Insisting on identifying policy outcomes seriously complicates the research task at hand.

The outcomes one wishes to measure are themselves usually less well-defined than policy outputs. Environmental outcomes are notoriously difficult to agree on and measure. Has air quality in the United States improved over the past thirty years? It depends on what you measure (say, conventional pollutants like ozone versus hazardous air pollutants), when you measure it (many techniques were not used until recently, so longitudinal data are not available), and where (some parts of the country are cleaner, others dirtier). Moreover, what would air quality be like if the U.S. public and private sectors had *not* spent some $30 billion on emissions controls over the last few decades? How much easier it is, then, simply to tot up the dollars spent by industry and the EPA, to catalogue the programs adopted and the number of personnel in and out of government working on environmental management, and to use these to gauge regulatory successes.

In open space battles, there is a big difference between what environmentalists want and what they actually get. In other words, a lot can go wrong between policy outputs and policy outcomes. Along the way, local leaders make more or less concerted attempts to mobilize action, suggest alternatives, and broker deals. Real estate markets ebb and flow, sometimes prompting landowners to speculate wildly on possible zoning changes and, at other times, motivating landholders to shed properties quickly, even at a loss, which can open a window of opportunity for bargain-basement preservation.

DEFINING AND MEASURING OPEN SPACE

Local land use decisions may or may not have a direct effect on what landscapes look like, what functions they provide, and what potential they bequeath to future generations. Consequently, I treat policy outputs and outcomes separately. Policy outputs are manifestations of local willingness and ability to protect land, but they may differ from what actually happened on the ground. Therefore, I consider indicators of outputs (money, personnel, legislation) as *independent* variables so that I avoid conflating outputs and outcomes. To eliminate some of the complexities of defining and measuring policy outcomes, I define open space as land purchased by local governments or conservation land trusts; thus, in this book I seek to explain patterns of land *acquisition*. More formally, I choose land acreages acquired in fee simple title (i.e., outright ownership), by local agencies or organizations as my principal dependent variable. These lands are either transferred to government agencies or managed by the preserving group.

I focus on land acquisition because I am skeptical of nonacquisition means of protecting land. As John Wright points out, land use regulation and planning have not been very successful at conserving land, for two reasons. First, "land-use regulations focus on how land will be developed, not if it should be. The essential purpose of regulation is, therefore, not to conserve land but to see that developments are of the desired type and density, that design criteria are met, that local infrastructure can handle the increased load" (1993, p. 11). Second, "many private landowners make shortsighted, environmentally damaging land development decisions driven by a desire for profit." They react strongly to planning programs partly "because they tend to believe that God and the Constitution have bestowed on them the absolute right to use their land in any way they choose, even if such use would be obviously and significantly injurious to their neighbors. Thus, land-use regulation is widely seen as an anti-American, un-Godly 'taking' of basic rights" (ibid., p. 12). Lands that are wholly owned by a local government or land trust are much less susceptible to being developed than lands that sit in an area delimited as a greenbelt or zoned for agriculture.

Despite the problems inherent in regulatory approaches, some properties are preserved without being purchased, by important mechanisms such as conservation easements and restrictive zoning. However, these mechanisms often represent lower-order protection, with easements representing more secure protection than zoning. In addition, systematically measuring easement or zoning activity across many jurisdictions is a far more difficult and uncertain task than counting acreage.

Gathering land ownership statistics at the substate level is a challenge. No state agency holds centralized records of all public land ownership in California. However, using the *California Parks and Recreation Society Annual Directory* and other local government sourcebooks, I was able to survey approximately six hundred local government entities known to have parks and recreation or open space agencies.[2]

Of California's fifty-eight counties, eleven (Alpine, Del Norte, Inyo, Mariposa, Modoc, Mono, Plumas, Sierra, Siskiyou, Trinity, and Tuolumne) are almost entirely in federal ownership and stand outside the "normal" pattern of preservation by local agencies and organizations. In these eleven counties there is little opportunity for local governments or land trusts to purchase private land for public open space. This book thus covers park and open space parcels in the remaining forty-seven counties. I ignore parcels smaller than 10 acres on the assumption that many of these are tot lots for small children and municipal sports and fairground facilities. Such parks are important to the neighborhood life of large and small cities, but they do not represent major commitments to nature-oriented recreation and preservation on the urban fringe.

LOCAL OPEN SPACE PRESERVATION PATTERNS AND USES

Once we assess the number of acres acquired by local preservationists, we can begin to look for geographic, institutional, and temporal patterns of land preservation in California. Is preserved land widespread and relatively uniform in distribution, or is it idiosyncratic and varied? Is it used for recreation, habitat protection, or growth management?

Many hundreds of times local communities and their leaders indeed succeeded in setting aside valuable land that stood in the way of the bulldozer. Counting only lands wholly owned by cities, counties, and special districts, we find that local actors have acquired a little over 570,000 acres since the 1920s. Adding in gifts to the state parks system that were acquired or brokered largely by local actors, and lands acquired by local land trusts, that figure rises to as much as 1.2 million acres. This amount may not appear large relative to California's total acreage (about 101 million acres) or to federal land in the state (about 46 million acres, or 45.5 percent of California's land area),[3] but it is on a par with what the California Department of Parks and Recreation has acquired and managed during this period (about 1.3 million acres).

Counties vary widely with respect to the number and size of tracts of open space protected by local efforts, amounting to anywhere from a few dozen acres to more than 90,000 acres (see figure 3 and appendix 1). The variation is also striking when viewed as a per capita phenomenon: from zero acres per thousand residents to about 200 acres per thousand residents. As a proportion of a county's area, local open space ranges from much less than 1 percent to more than 12 percent. Figure 4 shows county preservation as a combination (or "index" in statistical terms) of total acres, acres as a percent of county area, and acres protected per 1,000 residents. Figures 3 and 4 show that the more urbanized coastal counties (Santa Clara, Marin, Alameda, Orange) appear to be the ones most ag-

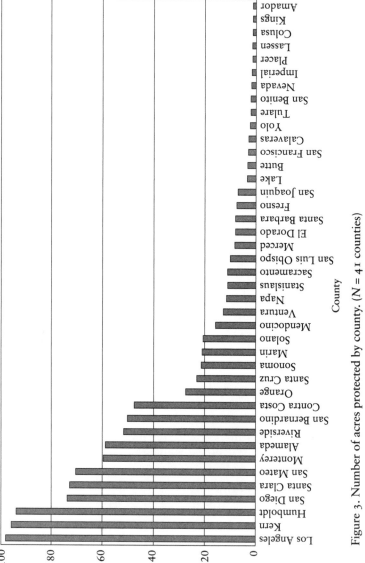

Figure 3. Number of acres protected by county. ($N = 41$ counties)

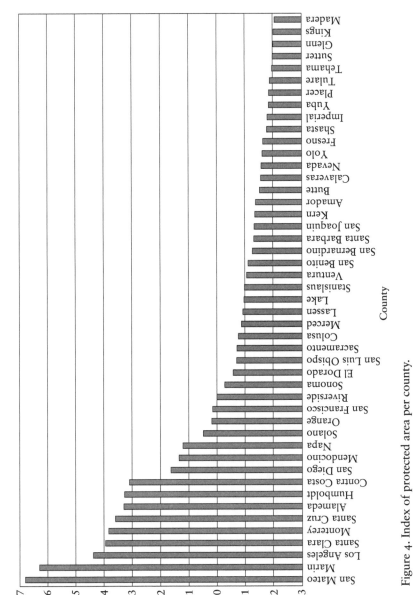

Figure 4. Index of protected area per county.

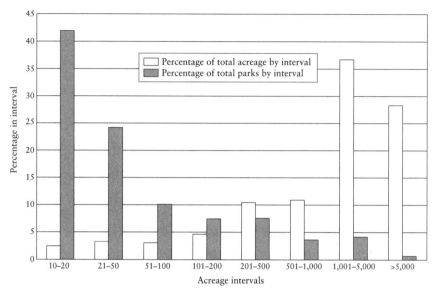

Figure 5. Distribution of park acreage held by local governments, statewide.

gressively protecting open space near their big cities, and that some preservation occurs in the valley counties that have larger urban centers.

Considering only city, county, and special parks and recreation agencies in my forty-seven-county sample, I found that about 400 jurisdictions hold slightly more than 2,700 parks that are 10 acres or larger. Cities hold about 147,000 acres in approximately 1,800 parks, which have an average size of 82 acres. Counties hold a little under twice the acreage of cities: about 241,000 acres held in about 500 parks, which have an average size of 482 acres. Special parks and recreation districts hold about 183,000 acres in 489 parcels, which have an average size of 373 acres. Figure 5 shows the distributions of local park acreages. Most of the parks are small, but most of the acreage is contained in the relatively few large parks.

Land trusts are also important. These private organizations rely largely on donations or grants from members, nonmembers, foundations, and state and federal government to protect land. At the close of the twentieth century, about 120 land trusts were active in California. Land trusts have helped preserve approximately 250,000 acres through fee simple acquisition and another 91,000 acres under conservation easements. They have also protected, mostly through acquisition, another

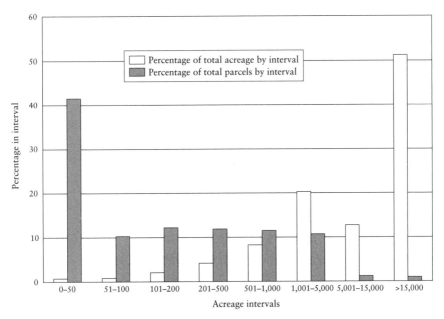

Figure 6. Distribution of open space acreage held by land trusts, statewide.

230,000 acres that have been subsequently transferred to state and federal landholders, for a total of about 571,000 acres.

Approximately 600 parcels comprise these land trust acres. Figure 6 demonstrates that land trusts, mirroring local government, tend to protect fairly large pieces of land. Over 83 percent of the land trust acreage is held in parcels that are 1,000 acres or larger. Thus land trust efforts, like those of local and regional parks agencies, serve a wide variety of needs, including watershed and habitat protection, urban growth management, and recreation.

Most of the acreage protected by private trusts has involved fewer than twenty-five organizations. Just twenty of these acquired well over a third of the acreage protected by local, private trusts in California. However, adding in the contributions by organizations operating statewide—such as the Trust for Public Land, the Nature Conservancy, and the Save-the-Redwoods League—*doubles* the privately protected acreage in California.

Local open space preservation in California is a widespread phenomenon that continued steadily throughout the twentieth century. Perfectly commensurable data collected over time are not available, but for rough comparison, Samuel T. Dana and Myron Krueger estimated that county and municipal parkland holdings in California amounted to approximately 260,000 acres in 1957 (1958, p. 105). Twenty years later, Donald Ito (1977) inventoried local public landholders and found that regional parks (greater than 15 acres each) totaled 472,890 acres. A 1987 survey conducted by the state Department of Parks and Recreation estimated that local governments held 568,348 acres of parks of all sizes, including very small municipal sports and recreation fields (California Department of Parks and Recreation 1988).

At present, cities, counties, special districts, and land trusts continue to arrange successfully for the purchase and transfer of substantial acreage. In the San Francisco Bay Area and environs alone, the establishment of regional parks and open space districts spanned the twentieth century. The extensive holdings of the East Bay Regional Parks District (in the San Francisco Bay Area) were secured in Contra Costa and Alameda Counties beginning in the early 1930s. In 1934, at a time when the regional water district was divesting itself of watershed lands, county residents put on the ballot (and approved, with 72 percent in favor) an initiative to buy expensive ridge-top lands with property taxes (Olmsted Brothers and Hall 1984). Rather strikingly, the vast majority of voters in these two semiurban counties voted to tax themselves—during the Great Depression—to preserve open space. Further south, park and open space acquisition has had a long history in Santa Clara County (home of Silicon Valley) too: the county parks department was created in 1956, the Midpeninsula Regional Open Space District in 1972 (with strong advisory approval from voters), and the Santa Clara Open Space Authority in 1994 (also with strong advisory approval from voters).

Local governments energetically continue to acquire and protect land. For example, data on the nine counties of the San Francisco Bay Area show that, as of 1998, collectively they had set aside some 265,000 acres through primarily local efforts, with nearly 50,000 acres of these—just about 19 percent—having been acquired since 1988 (State of California 1969–1996.). Similarly, California's special districts have been consistently active. The 154 special districts entrusted with a parks and recreation mandate spent over $1 billion (in 1999 dollars) in land acquisition costs alone between 1969 and 1996.[4] These expenditures vary from year to year, but, with an average of $37 million spent per year, a little over half of the spending occurred since 1982. Inadequate local government records make it impossible to tell just how many acres were protected in each of the past fifty years. However, anecdotal evidence suggests that the big surges occurred in the mid-1960s and mid-1970s. From the mid-

1980s onward, local preservationists have steadily acquired substantial acreage.

Local governments and land trusts alike acquire and manage their parks and open space to meet multiple, often conflicting, uses. Table 1 lists these uses and the typical parcel sizes associated with different park purposes. The open space acreages and size classes depicted in figures 3–6 serve the different purposes listed in the table.

By almost any measure, local open space preservation efforts represent an impressive accomplishment. However, the aggregate data mask the land use struggles fought parcel by parcel, decade by decade. Usually, preservationists lose more than they gain, if the history of development, and habitat, wetland, and agricultural land loss, is any indication.

THE POLICY CAPACITY MODEL

Despite the difficulty, open space has been preserved by local effort time and again, from the redwood forests in the coastal north to the desert in the southeast. In some parts of California, preservation began early in the twentieth century and continues today. The physical and temporal patterns of local open space preservation tell us where land is protected, which regions are better represented, and which institutions appear to be most successful. But why and how does land preservation happen? Why do preservation attempts consistently succeed in some places, while in others preservation barely reaches the status of a pressing issue? Questions of this general nature—essentially concerning variations in local policies, outcomes, capacities, and social choices—have interested practitioners (specifically, legislators and planners) and social scientists alike for years (Boyne 1985, 1992; Brace and Jewett 1995; Lester and Lombard 1990; Rice and Sumberg 1997; Ringquist 1993; Sharpe and Newton 1984; Stonecash 1996).

A community's *policy capacity* is its ability and willingness to respond to public problems and opportunities. Understanding why some communities mount considerably more comprehensive social or environmental programs than others do is important for ensuring equitable access to these benefits. Policy capacity comparisons help policy makers and scholars learn how innovations arising in some local governments diffuse to others.

The few studies that do focus on environmental protection outcomes, and not just policy outputs, use explanatory models that rely on both socioeconomic and political variables.[5] For example, Evan J. Ringquist

TABLE 1. PARKS AND OPEN SPACE USES AND SIZES

Use	Typical size (acres)	Facilities	Management issues
Active recreation Sports facilities Water recreation sites Recreational, historical, and cultural centers Environmental–natural history interpretation, science education centers	1–50	Usually requires developed facilities	Often requires considerable management costs and personnel
Passive recreation Hiking Camping Bird-watching, ecotourism Picnicking	5–100	Largely undeveloped facilities	Requires management for trail maintenance and access Growing conflicts between recreationists and habitat conservation, especially over use of trails by pedestrians versus off-road vehicles, horses, and mountain bikes
Nonuse Watershed protection (groundwater recharge, erosion prevention) Flood control Urban growth management, greenbelt function Agricultural land preservation Wildlife habitat preservation	100–1,000+	Rarely includes developed facilities	Requires substantial management costs, especially where fire management, fencing, restoration, or grazing are included in the regime Property edges vulnerable to encroachment by active users and neighbors

integrated political-economic characteristics (such as wealth and political ideology), group influence (such as organized interests), and political system characteristics (in this case, a professional legislature) to examine variations in state air and water quality (1993, pp. 88–93). Ringquist purposefully sought to understand not only how these political and economic variables affected the decisions adopted by state environmental-policy makers but also how air and water quality in the state improved or degraded as a function of those decisions. He found that economic wealth is not a dominant factor in either air or water quality regulation, and that strong regulatory programs did make a difference in controlling air pollution and, to a lesser extent, water pollution.

David H. Folz and Joseph M. Hazlett tested whether recycling programs are equally effective in "communities located in different regions, whose populations vary in size, socioeconomic composition, political culture, and form of government." One of their dependent variables was estimated waste diversion, which allowed them to measure an environmental outcome more directly. They found that the variation in successful recycling efforts from city to city was best explained by "the specific recycling policies adopted, the process by which communities made these policy decisions, and other features related to the program's operation" (Folz and Hazlett 1991, pp. 526, 531).

For explanatory and heuristic purposes, a successful model of policy capacity should permit researchers to both integrate all theoretically plausible and reasonably obtainable independent variables and describe the mechanism by which these affect environmental outcomes. The policy capacity model I use in this book is founded on the premise that some communities are more capable than others of mounting environmental protection activities. Such communities support local leaders with political, economic, and technical resources necessary for sustaining and implementing environmental programs.

I define "environmental policy capacity" as a community's ability to engage in collective action that secures environmental public goods and services. The model is integrative, relying on three major components that each contribute to a community's environmental problem-solving ability (I summarize these factors in general terms here and specify their measures in later chapters). First are the resources and constraints *internal* to the policy system, such as local revenues and administrative expertise. Second, a community's civic resources, such as voluntarism and political engagement, are vital factors influencing both mobilization and policy implementation. Third, communities marshal their policy capacity in response to *external* constraints and resources, such as the degree of development pressure facing a given jurisdiction, the nature of state or federal mandates and funding, and the particular landscape features that may motivate special consideration. If we think of policy capacity as a sort of currency, consideration of external constraints and resources reminds us that the buying power of a dollar varies depending on where you live. To extend the analogy, policy capacity resources provide the incentive and reward for political leadership in open space protection. Leaders draw on their community values; their successes serve to reinvest in local resources.

Note the expansion in the term "policy." A classic definition of public policy is "a course of governmental action or inaction in response to social problems" that states a government's "intent to achieve certain goals and objectives through a conscious choice of means, usually within some specified period" (Vig and Kraft 1994, p. 5). Policy here refers to a community's set of collective choices and actions, particularly as these affect outcomes. An important element of policy capacity is a community's ongoing posture toward, and its responses to, social problems and opportunities. Such postures and responses can be captured in measures of civic engagement and attitudes toward government and public goods. In this sense, policy is as much an orientation and an action agenda as it is a decision formally taken by government agents.

My policy capacity model goes beyond the political-capacity or capability terms usually used in political science research. When referring to policy capacity, political scientists usually mean either the capability of the state to deliver policy outputs that raise and spend funds for given programs, or the particular intellectual and psychological endowments of individual citizens (in their role as political participants or potential participants). In the former category, for example, David B. Robertson and Dennis R. Judd define government policy-making capacity as the ability to "entertain a variety of responses to social and economic problems, to enact or reject authoritative solutions, and to implement its decisions" (1989, p. 9). Ann O'M. Bowman and Richard Kearney, quoting Honadle (1981), define capacity as "the ability to anticipate and influence change; make informed, intelligent decisions about policy; develop programs to implement policy; attract and absorb resources; manage resources; and evaluate current activities to guide future actions" (Bowman and Kearney 1988, p. 342).

R. Kent Weaver and Bert A. Rockman refer to government capability as "a pattern of government influence on its [local] environment that produces substantially similar outcomes across time and policy areas" (1993, p. 6). The specific capabilities they assessed involved a government's ability to set and maintain policy priorities, especially in the face of opposition by powerful, organized interests. Highly capable governments, in Weaver and Rockman's terms, could also effectively design and implement public policies under conditions of political conflicts and cleavages.

One definition that focuses on the competence of individual citizens asserts that capacity is "the overall ability of an individual to take part in the political process. This incorporates a practical dimension (the knowledge necessary to know how to participate), a psychological dimension (the belief that one can influence the system), and an experiential dimension (the drawing of lessons from activity in politics that makes one believe it is worth participating again)" (Berry et al. 1993, p. 257). Similarly, for Anne Schneider and Helen Ingram, capacity essentially refers to adequate knowledge and fiscal resources, which can then translate into program expenditures or staffing. For example, capacity-building policy tools "provide information, training, education, and resources to enable individuals, groups, or agencies to make decisions or carry out activities" (1990, p. 517).

My policy capacity model relies on both types of capability: that of government, in its execution of official duties, and that of civil society, in its pursuit of collective action (whether perceived by participants as political mobilization or not).[6] To be useful to the study of politics and society, the policy capacity model must propose a mechanism by which the many factors discussed above come together to effect changes in outcomes. I envision a relatively simple model of policy capacity and performance in the open space context (see figure 7), much like Robert Putnam's 1993 conception of institutional performance.

Local environmental policy capacity exists in a particular setting, such as a city, county, region, during a given time period, such as a particular decade. As shown in figure 7, the setting is subject to constraints and resources external to city or county policy systems. Cities and counties may have relatively abundant lands still in private agriculture or open space, or undeveloped lots may be few and far between. Similarly, some parts of California have relatively more compelling landscapes—rivers, foothills, canyons, deserts, forests—that motivate preservationists. The state and federal governments also act as powerful factors external to local policy systems, sometimes by providing funding for environmental programs, and at other times by appropriating local revenues for state purposes.

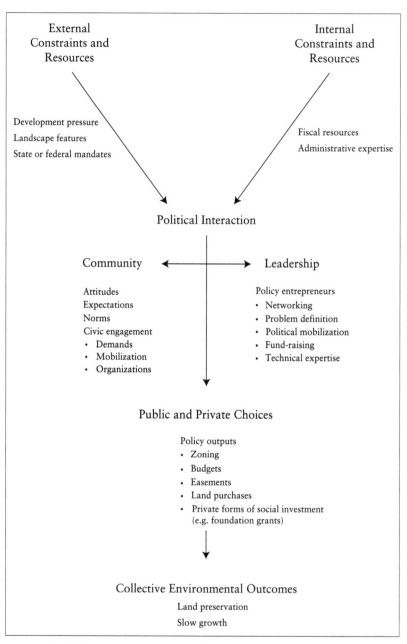

External
Constraints and
Resources

Internal
Constraints and
Resources

Development pressure
Landscape features
State or federal mandates

Fiscal resources
Administrative expertise

Political Interaction

Community ← → Leadership

Attitudes
Expectations
Norms
Civic engagement
• Demands
• Mobilization
• Organizations

Policy entrepreneurs
• Networking
• Problem definition
• Political mobilization
• Fund-raising
• Technical expertise

Public and Private Choices

Policy outputs
• Zoning
• Budgets
• Easements
• Land purchases
• Private forms of social investment
  (e.g. foundation grants)

Collective Environmental Outcomes

Land preservation

Slow growth

Figure 7. Model for policy capacity and land preservation.

Internal constraints and resources consist of local fiscal revenues and administrative resources. While sales- and property-tax formulas vary little throughout California, communities vary quite a bit in their ability to raise local funds, either because they attract a different tax base or because they have greater or lesser public support for ballot-box financing of bonds, taxes, and fees. The constraints and resources depicted in figure 7 set the context for political interaction between community residents and local leaders. These policy constraints and opportunities directly affect the policy system, especially by changing the relationship between local desires and local expectations. For example, local desire for growth management may be tempered by low or heavily encumbered tax revenues or by state and federal limitations on taxation, such as Proposition 13, or by land use restrictions, such as U.S. Supreme Court takings cases.[7]

The second capacity factor is the local level of civic resources, generally speaking, and civic environmentalism, in particular. Local civic environmentalism reflects public expectations concerning the provision of environmental goods. Collective norms strongly influence a policy system composed of formal political structures, such as county governments and city hall, nongovernmental organizations, and private individuals. In the model of a community with great environmental policy capacity, the social norm is to expect a high level of environmentally sound individual behavior and institutional performance. The second factor interacts with the policy entrepreneurship of a given community. Policy entrepreneurship can come from both public and private sectors but is fundamentally aimed at affecting public sector choices and management.

Thus, the policy capacity model suggests that, when citizens have high expectations for the policy system, they provide the political and moral rewards that support environmental protection and environmentally sensitive choices. These choices produce collective environmental goods and services, or "on the ground" outcomes.

Based on this model, one would expect policy capacity in the environmental context to be highest where

- environmental conditions and problems are locally visible;
- local budgetary, technical, and administrative resources are relatively high (administrative and economic resources);
- the community greatly desires, and has high expectations of, institutional performance in environmental protection (environmental preferences enable policy choices);[8]

· political leaders sustain a commitment to environmental policy
  and programs (entrepreneurship acts upon community resources).

USING THE POLICY CAPACITY MODEL

If these capacity elements strongly shape policy outcomes, what are the
observable implications of the policy capacity model? If the model is accu-
rate, communities that exhibit relatively more general pro-environmental
sympathy (from residents and local leaders) and have access to relatively
greater resources (either public or private, in terms of time, expertise, or
funding) should engage in greater local environmental protection activities. It is unlikely that all policy capacity components will be present or
absent in any given community. Instead, a community exhibiting strong
environmental protection behavior might compensate for low levels of
one component, such as public fiscal resources, with high levels of
another, such as political commitment or civic voluntarism in environmental programs. Similarly, where general civic engagement is low, one
might expect environmental activism—as well as mobilization against
environmental protection—to be relatively absent. In such a situation,
private leadership, local revenues, and administrative capabilities could
be the principal contributors to local environmental programs.

I also expect communities to react to differences in the material conditions facing them. As I will elaborate later, communities will not feel
compelled to spend scarce resources on land acquisition unless the negative effects of urban sprawl—and the remedies, which may only sometimes include preservation—are fairly obvious. Of course, California's
residents see what is going on. They understand that commute times
have lengthened, that new pavement lies where orchards and farms
recently existed, that access to the San Joaquin and Sacramento Rivers
has become difficult, and that every hot summer day in any of the major
urban areas stands a good chance of being smoggy. But it is not enough
that the problems exist. Many problems continue unabated year after
year. For development and growth to become recognized problems, residents must see them as such, as well as have the social and institutional
means of proposing and implementing change.

Although the policy capacity model I use here was designed with land
use outcomes in mind, my intention is that it will have broader applications for studies of local governance. The model should be especially useful in exploring policy issues for which local performance is highly
discretionary, relatively unregulated by the state or federal governments,

and highly susceptible to the kinds of political and economic resources that vary locally. Thus, water conservation, waste management, discretionary educational programs, and local mass transit infrastructure could all be analyzed through a policy capacity lens.

METHODS

Conducting any inquiry into California's environment and institutions demands a diverse approach. While complex, California's tumultuous history is well documented with quantitative and qualitative data. Perhaps because its professional legislature and bureaucracy were created early relative to the state's late entry into the union, and funded relatively well, California has collected valuable fiscal and environmental data for many years. This enabled me to be opportunistic in this study, to draw on any data and observations I felt would provide further insights into open space preservation. Multivariate analyses allow me to set the stage on which my interview respondents act out their stories. As Putnam puts it, "Our contrasting impressions . . . must be confirmed, and our theoretical speculations disciplined, by careful counting" (1993, p. 12). In-depth interviews with dozens of local respondents immersed me and my research assistants in the rich detail of local efforts to struggle with thorny land use dilemmas.

My primary unit of analysis is the county. Counties exercise a great deal of land use authority (especially over unincorporated lands), and parks agencies or land trusts often operate at the county scale. California's counties are also quite large, sometimes encompassing several watersheds, metropolitan areas, habitats, and other landscape features. Of course, much land preservation occurs at a very small scale; accordingly, I report on several illustrative community-level examples that convey a sense of the unique nature of every land preservation effort.

Given that much of California's local open space has been acquired steadily over the years since 1960, I collected quantitative data back into the 1960s, when possible, and mined newspaper archives and agency files back several decades whenever available. What emerges in the chapters ahead draws on the following sources:

- Dozens of interviews with local planners, open space activists, local elected officials, and agency staff conducted over a period of five years.
- A telephone survey of 4,100 California residents, most of whom

lived in three multicounty regions and the twenty-seven most
populous counties. The survey assessed residents' views about
the role and performance of their local government, the importance of parks and open space, and respondents' civic behavior.
This large sample size allowed me to take stock of county-level
differences in civic engagement, voluntarism, environmental
policy support, and political ideology, especially concerning
the importance of public goods and services.

· Nine main sources provided measurements on my other independent variables, which quantified fiscal and administrative
resources, environmental policy support, local development
pressure, and landscape features. To collect fiscal data, I recorded
local government revenues for cities, counties, and special districts
from the California Department of Finance's annual statistical
abstract. The Governor's Office of Research and the state Department of Parks and Recreation provided valuable data on administrative capacity. I used local returns on statewide environmental
ballot propositions to measure environmental policy preferences
at the local level. The U.S. Census of Agriculture, the California
State Board of Equalization, and the state's Farmland Mapping
and Monitoring Project and Department of Finance provided data
that enabled me to assess the level of development pressure each
of California's counties has faced over the past twenty-five years.
Landscape data consist of U.S. Geological Survey data on hydrographic features and county elevation. The census bureau's Topo-
logically Integrated Geographic Encoding and Referencing System
files permitted analyses of landscape features of riparian and elevation data.

OVERVIEW

In many respects this study documents an ongoing natural experiment
that is being replicated in many federalist systems of governance.
California and the federal government hold constant the macrolevel policy context to which local actors bring their energy, goals, and resources.
Accordingly, with its historical account of the changing state and federal
roles in this contentious policy arena, chapter 2 sets the stage for a discussion of local preservation. I use the policy capacity model to illustrate
the changes that occurred in local communities as California and federal

agencies first pushed cities and counties to jump on the environmental bandwagon, then abruptly left locals to implement expensive, complex mandates while state and federal policy makers withdrew funds and political support.

Chapters 3 and 4 apply the policy capacity model to local differences in open space throughout California. Together, these chapters reveal the enabling factors and policy contexts that policy entrepreneurs draw on to make open space preservation happen. Chapter 3 describes how development pressure, important landscape features, fiscal resources, and administrative resources prompt a preservationist response. It then assesses the variation in and importance of local government fiscal and administrative resources before and after the revolutionary Proposition 13 of 1978.

Chapter 4 examines the phenomenon of civic environmentalism. It assesses county variations in civic environmentalism using microlevel data (surveys of individuals) as well as macrolevel comparisons of voter support for environmental protection.

Chapter 5 analyzes the role of the policy entrepreneurs who drive the land protection deals. It shows how they draw on the resources described in chapters 3 and 4, along with a vision for protective land use in their communities.

In chapter 6, I develop a typology of the mechanisms by which local open space is acquired (by county) and assess the policy capacities of selected counties. I end the book with a look toward emerging issues and some policy implications of the study—should policy capacity be increased, and, if so, where and how? What are the roles for local, state, and federal governments and nongovernmental organizations?

My conclusions do not amount to a handbook for land preservation, but they do reflect on the possibility of sustainable communities, at least in regard to communities' land use choices. Sustainability and democracy are compatible at the local level, but making progress toward each presents a great challenge for the future. More generally, the land preservation story reveals local autonomy and agenda-setting in a policy area characterized by very high costs and low government revenues, truly a struggle against the odds.

CHAPTER 2

A Statewide History
of Local Preservation Efforts

From the Early 1900s to the Present

The East Bay communities face an unusual opportunity.
Nature has placed within easy reach of this growing region
a contiguous border of scenic land, most of which is too
rugged for industrial, or extensive residential purposes,
but possessed of a high recreational value.

Olmsted Brothers and Ansel F. Hall,
*Report on Proposed Park Reservations
for East Bay Cities, California, 1930*

The state's once-vigorous preservation leadership became moribund after
the 1970s, leaving local actors to fend for themselves as they challenged
the growth machine. The institutional opportunities available to promote land preservation, the constraints imposed by the state's on-and-off
promotion of land preservation, and the antitax crusade of 1978 all
shaped the policy context that local governments commonly face today.
This chapter illustrates the variety of community policy tools that
evolved in response to local or state opportunities and constraints; subsequent chapters show how and why communities would come to differ
in their responses.

The idea of regional open space is not new, but the ways in which
open space has come to be protected have changed significantly in the
past hundred years. I distinguish three historical periods of open space
protection. A top-down approach characterized the first period, beginning in the early 1900s, whereby mainly the elites and technocrats, often
in the state government, were responsible for initiating open space
preservation efforts. This period lasted through the first half of the twen-

tieth century, and it realized slow, steady land acquisitions, primarily for recreation purposes, often with the state government providing major funding.

The second period emerged during the late 1950s and early 1960s, as the first wave of the modern environmental movement swept through California. During this time, which lasted until the late 1970s, local, state, and federal funds for local open space preservation grew tremendously. The passage of the antitax Proposition 13 in 1978 initiated the end of this second period of open space protection. After Proposition 13 became law, large and reliable public budgets for land preservation disappeared. Coalitions of nongovernmental organizations became important initiators of open space protection, often choosing local ballot measures to challenge the growth machine. But antigovernment and antitax sentiments, coupled with the pro-growth Deukmejian administration, quashed a slow-growth trend that had spanned the 1970s. The third period began in the mid-1980s, as nongovernmental organizations matured and changed the debate from slow-growth to planned growth, and rebounded with a flood of ballot initiatives, many of them successful, to curb sprawl and protect open space. In the following sections, I discuss each of these historical periods within the context of the policy capacity model, focusing especially on changes in factors that affect policy capacity, including internal and external constraints and resources.

1900–1960: TOP-DOWN OPEN SPACE PRESERVATION

From the late nineteenth century onward, California's state and municipal leadership, landscape architects, and civic groups advanced bold, forward-thinking proposals for parks and open spaces on the urban fringe. Whereas Teddy Roosevelt's administration spurred federal landholders to create large national parks around the turn of the century (Andrews 1999), local, regional, and state governments began planning for their acquisitions in the 1920s and 1930s.

From a policy capacity perspective, a series of state mandates provided external constraints on and resources for local communities. The state legislature began requiring local governments to develop comprehensive general plans in 1927; it added new requirements in a piecemeal fashion, regulating land use and traffic circulation in 1955, housing in 1967, and conservation and open space in 1970 (Burby and May 1997, p. 28).

By means of these mandates, the state of California laid the ground-

work for many local open space preservation efforts undertaken up to
the early 1970s. It did so via three kinds of statutory thrusts, one
designed to increase local powers of land acquisition, another intended
to motivate voluntary conservation arrangements between landowners
and local governments, and a third aimed at increasing local government
planning capacity. To begin with, the state gradually defined and expanded the scope of local powers for land preservation. Starting in 1905
and extending well into the 1950s, the California state legislature passed
a series of statutes expressly granting cities and counties (and, later, special districts) powers they would need in order to acquire lands for park,
recreation, and open space purposes. These powers allowed local government to assess property taxes, condemn lands, and form special parks,
recreation, or open space districts.[1]

Later, the state legislature sought to motivate voluntary conservation
by private landowners through a series of statutes adopted over a twenty-
year period beginning in 1955. That year, the legislature attempted to
decrease development pressure on agriculture in Santa Clara County by
allowing farmers to choose to have their lands zoned exclusively for agriculture (the so-called Greenbelt Law of 1955); a Scenic Easement Deed
Act of 1959 followed. The thrust of these efforts was to permit (or prod)
local governments to assess private property at the lower rates associated
with lands set aside for agricultural or open space preservation, not at the
wildly soaring values of many exurban parcels.

The state legislature also helped cities, counties, and regions to
develop the necessary expertise for land use (and by extension, conservation) planning. As far back as 1927, the state allowed local governments
to form planning commissions.

In 1938, the state legislature began allocating 30 percent of tideland
oil royalties to state park acquisition and development. That figure rose
to 70 percent in 1943; the allocation was frozen from 1947 to 1954,
when the federal government impounded the royalties pending settle-
ment (in favor of the states) of disputes over tidelands jurisdiction
(USORRRC 1962).

Although the state never required plans for parks and other recreation
areas, local governments frequently developed plans for parks and open
space that subsequently informed city and county general-plan amendments. In most cases, the planners who wrote these reports identified
park and open space needs, often based on ratios of some given acreage
per thousand residents. Sometimes these formulas were quite modest: in
1948, Los Angeles County anticipated needing only about 1,900 acres to

meet a goal of 1.5 acres per thousand residents within a 1/2-to-1-mile radius. That goal was designed to provide playing fields and picnic areas in parks of 10–15 acres. Other plans, like those of the East Bay communities (located on the east side of San Francisco Bay), framed their acquisition goals in terms of protecting hillsides and watersheds or providing the kind of space that Charles Eliot termed in 1893 as that which "appears to be a wilderness of indefinite extent" (cited in Olmsted and Hall 1984).

Nonbinding recreation and open space plans are usually laden with laudable goals and urgent recommendations, many of which are never realized. But the extensive record left by park planners and advocates in the twentieth century's early decades reminds us of just how long it takes to implement an open space vision, even during economically good times and with public support. This time lag demonstrates the important difference between policy outputs, which express public and private choices, and policy outcomes—in terms of land actually preserved or growth actually restricted. Many of the recommendations made decades ago to create parks agencies or acquire lands were indeed implemented, but over a long period and at considerable expense.

The most comprehensive and important of these plans was the 1930 *Parks, Playgrounds, and Beaches for the Los Angeles Region,* prepared by the Olmsted Brothers and Bartholomew and Associates landscape architecture firms as commissioned by the Los Angeles Chamber of Commerce. The extensive report thoroughly documented existing recreation opportunities and future needs, but it was disowned and virtually denounced at its publication by chamber members themselves. They objected to the plan's recommendations for a special district with wide geographic coverage and broad powers, as well as the hefty price tag for park acquisition and development (Hise and Deverell 2000).

The point is not that the early-twentieth-century reports ultimately determined whether and how parks districts would be founded and lands acquired. They certainly provided useful guidance about where to direct resources. More important, they often legitimated the pursuit of open space preservation, garnered the endorsements of civic leaders, and helped turn aside opposition to what might be portrayed as irresponsible government growth. In some cases, reports and treatises on open space lent prestige to parks advocates (Luten 1984).

Early reports such as those by the Olmsted Brothers and Bartholomew (1930), Olmsted and Hall (1930), Monterey County (*Park and Recreation Plan,* 1944), and Los Angeles County (*Report on Master Plan of*

Parks, 1948) commented on the rapid growth of California's urban centers and the need for park acquisitions to keep pace with development. In that sense, development pressure was already motivating an increase in local environmental policy capacity. Landscape architects and planners alike also pointed out the public costs of sprawl as a justification for preservation, as in this reference to the Los Angeles basin: "Purely as a public problem the use of the steeper portions of the hills for residential uses may become, and in fact is likely to become, a burden on the public for development and for maintenance far greater than the proportionate share of public revenue from those particular areas would seem to justify" (Olmsted and Hall 1984, p. 13).

Similarly, the 1930 *Parks, Playgrounds, and Beaches* report warned of the dangers associated with floodplain development in the Los Angeles basin:

> The lowlands may be just as good as any other for providing spaciousness of open scenery for parks and parkways; and it ought to be relatively cheap to acquire. Because of the innocent look it has in dry weather, it is not as cheap as it ought to be. Between floods it looks pretty good for building purposes to those who never saw what storm water can do in this country. Unsuspecting purchasers, victims of their own ignorance, will fall into the traps laid for them by the sharp practice of ruthless promoters, and such lands will be cut up, sold, and occupied. Unfortunately, the burden of such wrong development does not fall on the purchaser alone, and scarcely ever on the vendor, but most heavily on the community at large. (Olmsted Brothers and Bartholomew and Associates 1930, p. 14)

Development pressure itself motivated considerable planning and mobilization efforts. When residents of Alameda and Contra Costa Counties learned that the East Bay Municipal Utility District was planning to sell several thousand acres of hillside watersheds, they worried that development would overwhelm their communities with traffic, construction, and new residents. Civic leaders in Alameda County commissioned the Olmsted and Hall report as a way of making the case for a new regional parks district that would buy up ridge-top lands on the east side of the San Francisco Bay. The 1930 report laid the groundwork for a successful 1934 ballot measure creating the East Bay Regional Parks District.

Marin County's 1943 *Master Recreation Plan* provided an analysis of the open space challenge that was to become nearly ubiquitous throughout the state as increasing populations created a demand for both more housing and more recreation areas: "For the last several years, the residents of Marin have watched the gradual withdrawal of recreation areas from public use, with increasing alarm. The need for conservation has been recognized by interested citizen groups. The recent construction of hundreds of new homes throughout the County to provide for the increase in population has decreased the amount of available lands for public recreation, and ironically enough has increased the need for them" (Marin County 1943, p. 5).

The recreation plan also recognized the opportunity for land preservation created by the tension between land speculation and county building restrictions: "Many lands being proposed for public acquisition were purchased by the present owners for speculation purposes. These lands cannot now be developed because of strict government restrictions on private construction, and, therefore, the owners of such properties would welcome the opportunity to relieve themselves of the financial burden and would consider themselves fortunate to gain the original investment" (ibid.). The plan then advocated the creation of regional parks and open space districts.

The city of San Diego's 1956 master plan of parks and recreation called for adding 400 acres of parks and open space and 87 miles of rights-of-way for parks and beaches. All this was to be accomplished by 1970. According to the plan, "When this program is accomplished, San Diego will be among the few cities of the United States that have solved the Park and Recreation problem" (City of San Diego 1956, p. 33). The problem San Diego referred to was "an urgent challenge," namely, to acquire parks and recreation sites before or at the time land is subdivided and to correct deficiencies in the city's then current offerings.

In the same year, Alameda County's general plan, which included a separate parks and recreation element, even more explicitly identified rapid development as a motivator of land acquisition: "On the east side of the Bay, for instance, urban development will result in a continuous and intermingled sprawl of houses, shops and industrial establishments from Richmond to San Jose unless the citizens working through their city and county governmental processes make successful efforts to guide and control conservation and physical development of the land" (Alameda County 1956, p. 8). Similarly, a 1958 statewide land use analysis by Dana and Krueger called on cities and counties to acquire additional lands for watershed protection and recreation within easy reach of urban residents' homes (p. 178).

The records left by park planners and administrators throughout most of the twentieth century clearly express a general desire for preservation as a means to an end sought by many for sound reasons extending beyond environmental protection. These old park plans also show that, in this issue area, the administrative capacity for open space preservation often preceded other elements of policy capacity, such as fiscal resources and mass mobilization.

Nongovernmental organizations also played a valuable role in the early days of open space protection. The origins of California's state parks system can be traced directly to local efforts on behalf of old-growth redwoods in the Santa Cruz Mountains. The Sempervirens Club (founded in 1900 and later renamed the Sempervirens Fund) prodded the state to purchase several thousand unlogged acres in Big Basin. That successful campaign set the stage for future acquisitions as well as prompted the development of a professional agency and corps dedicated to land preservation primarily for recreational purposes (Yaryan 1999). The successes of the Sempervirens Club also encouraged the founders of the Save-the-Redwoods League (1918), who mobilized particularly on behalf of redwood forest protection in the coastal counties north of San Francisco; the league grew into a remarkably successful fund-raising organization. Thus, the first half of the twentieth century saw slow, steady land acquisitions, primarily for recreation purposes, often with the state government providing major funding and elites or technocrats providing much of the leadership in open space protection.

EARLY 1960S THROUGH THE 1970S: THE FIRST SLOW-GROWTH ERA

In the early 1960s, a new kind of conservation group emerged, organized as much to slow or prevent urban sprawl as to conserve especially appealing landscapes or important resources (Rome 1998, pp. 261–62). The San Francisco Bay Area's Greenbelt Alliance is a good example of a group that formed initially in response to a specific project but then went on to tackle development on a sustained basis. In 1958, about thirty years after the Olmsted-Hall report, the East Bay Municipal Utility District was again considering a big sale of its watershed lands, this time around the San Pablo Reservoir. Dorothy Erskine, an affordable-housing advocate active in San Francisco, rallied her friends and colleagues to organize a group calling itself Citizens for Regional Recreation and Parks. The group established quick successes opposing development of Angel Island and construction of the San Pablo Reservoir, then went on to publish a newsletter, *Regional Exchange,* to report on development and planning issues in the San Francisco Bay region.

In 1969, Citizens for Regional Recreation and Parks became a non-profit, tax-exempt organization and renamed itself People for Open Space. Thirty years and another name change (to the Greenbelt Alliance) later, this development-watchdog group has an impressive record: it has challenged building projects throughout the region, published dozens of reports and maps, and held workshops and conferences on regional planning. In the 1990s, the Greenbelt Alliance vigorously pitched the value of conservation easements for both agricultural and open space preservation, as well as the value of ballot measures on growth controls.

Other nongovernmental organizations shared the Greenbelt Alliance's vision but operated on a national level, like the Trust for Public Land (TPL), or a statewide level, like the Planning and Conservation League (PCL). The Trust for Public Land's organizational innovation was to serve as a land broker that acquired lands only to resell them to preservation entities or parks agencies: "By offering landowners the tax advantages of selling to a nonprofit, the organization could purchase land at a charitable discount—receiving, in essence, a donation of land value from the owner. When TPL then transferred ownership of the land to a public agency, part of that donation of land value would pay TPL's transaction costs and forward its broader mission of acquiring land for public ownership" (TPL 1997, p. 3).

Like the Greenbelt Alliance before it, the TPL formed in response to an especially controversial development, that of Marincello, a community of 30,000 planned for the Marin Headlands north of San Francisco. The TPL scored its first major victory when the Golden Gate National Recreation Area, America's first, largest, and most visited urban park, was designated on October 27, 1972. Since 1972, the TPL has helped protect over 1.2 million acres nationally.

The Planning and Conservation League formed in 1965, galvanized by bold plans to fill in the San Francisco Bay. The PCL's ongoing two-pronged strategy consists of policy and planning analysis, in order to define conservation problems, and vigorous efforts to harness the state's legislative authority on behalf of growth controls and conservation, in order to push for solutions. Over the years, the PCL has developed a reputation as an effective organization on both accounts. Since 1980 the organization has been author of or partner in several high-profile, successful environmental-policy initiatives placed on the statewide ballot that cover issues from habitat protection to mass transit funding (Meral 2001).

While new preservation and slow-growth organizations were being founded, local, state, and federal funds for local open space preservation grew tremendously. During the 1960s, the state legislature passed a number of laws to encourage the protection of open space. These included the California Land Conservation Act of 1965 (the Williamson Act), the Quimby Act of 1965, and the Open-Space Easement Act of 1969, along with its 1974 and 1977 amendments (Barrett and Livermore 1983). The Williamson Act encouraged farmers to "enroll" their land in a conservation program, whereby they agreed to keep their land in agricultural or open space use for a minimum of ten years; in exchange, owners paid much lower property taxes. The Quimby Act allowed local governments to require that developers set aside a portion of their subdivisions as parks or open space, or pay fees for parkland acquisition and maintenance. But the most important planning requirement came as part of the new consciousness of the environmental movement, when, in 1970, the legislature required cities and counties to include "open-space elements" in their general plans.[2]

Open space preservation efforts continued to focus on setting aside recreation lands, with a few notable exceptions, such as federal wildlife refuges and portions of a few state parks. Newly developed geographic information systems were used by the state Parks and Recreation Information System to generate reports in the 1960s and 1970s, which constituted early attempts at distributing recreation resources of different types at varying distances from communities.

The federal government also played a role during this period, traditionally as a source of funding via two principal programs, the Land and Water Conservation Fund (LWCF) and the old Housing and Urban Development (HUD) grant program for open space near urban areas. Each program constituted a major source of funding for local governments in the 1960s and 1970s, but the HUD program ended in the mid-1970s and the LWCF was virtually unfunded for most of the 1980s and 1990s.[3]

Local governments exercised a newfound boldness to regulate land use and raise taxes on behalf of environmental interests. Parks and open space reports and plans written after 1970 became even more explicit about the ills of urban sprawl, the cost of public infrastructure, and the loss of agricultural lands, rare plant communities, and wetlands. Even fairly cautious documents such as plans written by the state Department of Parks and Recreation clearly faulted urbanization, shortsighted local zoning, and population pressures for degrading wildland resources and limiting access to outdoor recreation (Cal DPR 1982, 1993).

But while environmentalism grew in California, so did sprawl. This conflict became apparent throughout the state as periods of proliferating exurban development were followed by citizen revolts against the growth machine. Several cities and towns succeeded in slowing growth, but the results were hardly felt on a regional basis. Instead, development leap-frogged to less restrictive jurisdictions, thereby aggravating regional congestion and the jobs-housing imbalance. Rapid growth and the environmental movement collided in the early 1970s, ushering in a first wave of slow-growth politics and policies throughout California. Appealing to residents' concerns about infrastructural burdens and the loss of distinctive, small-town character, slow-growth proponents drafted measures typically limiting the number of new units that could be permitted in a given jurisdiction each year.

In response to sprawl, open space plans and reports not only called for particular acquisitions but also made numerous institutional recommendations, as exemplified by events in Santa Clara County. As residents of the San Francisco East Bay Area had done a decade earlier when they formed the Citizens for Regional Recreation and Parks, a small group of west county residents got together in the late 1960s to form a land use watchdog organization, the Committee for Green Foothills. They came from the ranks of Stanford University alumni, professionals, and descendants of farming and ranching families. As is so often the case, proposed road and housing developments prompted them to delve into the arcana of land use planning and policy making. They found almost no truly protective land use controls. That is, many cities and counties in California of the late 1960s and early 1970s were either sluggishly revising their general plans, constantly granting variances and exceptions, or simply ignoring the environmental and economic implications of their generous permitting processes.

As Lennie Roberts of the Committee for Green Foothills explains, "We were formed in response to a threat that Palo Alto was going to develop from the current limits of Palo Alto all the way up to Skyline [Boulevard]. We were going to have a city of 60,000 people in the hills. And a number of people got together and decided, well, we'll be for something—we'll be for the Green Foothills."[4] Where the committee activists expected to find protections, either there were none or the political will to enforce them was absent. So Roberts and her friends set to work on several fronts. In addition to fighting for strong general plans and their implementation, they also recognized the need for landholding agencies with permanent sources of funds. But the committee was not the right organization for holding and managing land. It was avowedly and very publicly political. Committee members urging city councils and boards of supervisors to tighten land use and development restrictions would have received a cold reception from the county's larger landowners, many of whom were relatively conservative farmers, loggers, or ranchers. Landowners needed to be cultivated and approached by unthreatening, politically neutral organizations if preservationists were to succeed in pulling off conservation deals. Local governments might provide those neutral brokers.

In 1971, the landscape architecture firm Livingston and Blayney was commissioned by the city of Palo Alto to study its prospects for hillside development. A now famous conclusion of the report still cited decades later echoed the Olmsted and Hall report of 1930. It would be cheaper for local government and taxpayers to acquire and preserve open space in the Santa Cruz Mountains above Silicon Valley than to attempt extending infrastructure up the hillsides. The Committee for Green Foothills seized on the report's conclusions, taking them as an opportunity to expand the region's land preservation capacity. Roberts adds, "Based on a survey that we did, we decided it was time to form a district to buy the land and preserve it as open space. And, we also felt that it was kind of late in the game in 1972 to start doing this. The East Bay Regional Parks District had been in existence since the . . . thirties." Committee members went on to work with county supervisors, environmentalists, and state legislators to create the Midpeninsula Regional Open Space District. Roberts remembers,

> Since I grew up in the East Bay and used to look out at all this great land that they own, I used to think, "If only we had some more of these kinds of districts around." . . . So the idea wasn't new, but it was meant to be complementary to the county park system. And it was always a big political struggle to get the county Board of Supervisors that always had many, many other demands on their money to focus on buying more parklands. So it was partly due to government's lack of responsiveness that we decided to form this new district; . . . it was politically a good time to do it. It was the same year that the Monterey County Open Space District and Marin [County Open Space District] was formed.

1978: THE ANTITAX CRUSADE AND THE END OF THE FIRST SLOW-GROWTH MOVEMENT

No observer of local government in California can ignore the fiscal chaos visited upon cities and counties in the wake of the 1978 Proposition 13. The predominant political and institutional context for public policy turned inside-out with the passage of Proposition 13, from resource abundance and policy experimentation to stop-gap management. Local government revenues plummeted, from about $10 billion just prior to Proposition 13 to approximately half that amount shortly thereafter (Cal DPR 1994, 87).[5] Shortly after, in 1979, Proposition 4 placed a ceiling on both state and local government expenditures.

Proposition 13 began an era of tightfisted state and local fiscal policies in California in which cities and counties were motivated to adopt the land use policies most likely to replenish their depleted budgets. Thus, cities have zoned for high-sales-tax businesses, such as those found in malls, and have annexed open space and farmland to add new properties to their tax base (Ladd 1998; Schrag 1998).

In the absence of large and reliable public budgets for land preservation, local coalitions of environmentalists, farmers, and home owners challenged the state's powerful growth machine three times between the late 1960s and the late 1990s. Slow-growth activists quickly settled on the initiative and referendum as the tools of choice for restricting and containing development. Well over one hundred ballot measures attempting to impose urban growth boundaries or limit lines have been on local ballots since 1971 (Center for California Studies 1994–1997; Pincetl 1999; Porter 1987).

By 1982, the first slow-growth era was over. There were certainly more efforts to limit sprawl through the early 1980s, but activity had slowed to a trickle. Slow growth had been hampered by concerns over a sluggish economy, by the antigovernment sentiment embodied by Proposition 13, by Governor George Deukmejian's and President Ronald Reagan's administrations, and by the growth machine's newly developed sophistication in battling its opponents.

THE MID-1980S: PLANNED GROWTH EMERGES

Throughout the 1980s and 1990s the state remained absent from the slow-growth battle. There were certainly legislative attempts to enter the fray, but these amounted to little more than exhortation and study (Pincetl 1999). Governor Deukmejian's spending cuts mirrored the Reagan administration's rollback of conservation funding. Public and private actors alike became more innovative at cultivating public support for open space preservation. New strategies and a second planned-growth era emerged in the mid-1980s, when communities were compelled to greatly increase their reliance on ballot measures in the face of a superheated building boom.

But at the same time, the antitax crusade that started with Proposition 13 continued with Propositions 62 in 1986 and 218 in 1996. These ballot measures extended the supermajority-approval requirement of Proposition 13 to virtually all the types of assessments, fees, or taxes used by local governments.

From an electoral perspective, the antitax initiatives dramatically decreased the number of local measures with revenue-raising objectives that could pass. Slow-growth advocates made more frequent appeals to the electorate's sense of rationality and fair play. The 1986 elections saw no fewer than forty-five slow-growth measures on the ballot, about half of which passed.

Between 1986 and 1998, seventy-eight tax and bond acts for parks and open space were put on local ballots around the state. Of these, forty-eight (or 61.5 percent) received a better than 50 percent vote in favor, but because of Proposition 13's requirement for a supermajority of votes, only thirteen (16.6 percent) of the measures actually went into effect.[6]

Recreation was no longer the key focus of open space protection. Beginning in the 1980s, statewide ballot measures had habitat and wildlife protection goals, often explicitly earmarking substantial funds for acquisition and management of particularly valuable ecosystems. This second slow-growth era was also characterized by efforts to link development limits to a community's ability to absorb newcomers. In 1985, David Dowal, then acting director of the Institute for Urban and Regional Development at the University of California, Berkeley, pointed out that "the new model [of growth-control ballot measures] is more sophisticated in the sense that it's trying to link growth to capacity, whereas in the old days we just picked a magic number [for annual limits on new construction]" (Diringer 1985). Sewage, schools, transportation, and even parks infrastructure henceforth would need to keep pace with development. Debates now were less about growth versus no-growth and more about "plans versus no plans" (McCulloch 1989). Expensive public infrastructure was also a major reason voters in Milpitas and other California cities adopted ballot measures locking undeveloped hillsides out of urban service boundaries or into restrictive, low-density zoning ordinances (Wolverton 1998).

By the early 1990s, the challenge mounted by slow-growth advocates had cooled considerably in the face of heavy opposition from construction and allied industries. During the recession at that time, California was actually losing more residents than it was gaining, and the state's economic recovery appeared to be lagging behind that of the rest of the country. Construction was down, and many home owners lost money between 1989 and 1992.

In 1995, development pressure began building and citizen groups once again challenged it. Dozens of slow-growth measures appeared on local ballots between 1996 and 2000, and state and federal leaders peppered their campaigns with the rhetoric of "smart growth," "sustainable communities," and "livable cities."

Slow-growth ballot measures in the 1990s incorporated a decidedly populist air: instead of merely limiting the number of new units permitted or tying development to infrastructure, activists and their friends on city councils angrily attempted to require voter approval for any medium- to large-size new developments. Ballots in the Northern California cities of Pleasanton and San Ramon would have required voter approval of new developments with as few as ten units. The new measures were not successful, though some failed by only the slimmest of margins. However, certain measures designed to limit sprawl did succeed: by 1998, twenty-one counties and seventy-four cities had adopted urban growth boundaries or limit lines (California Governor's Office of Research 1999).

Activist organizing had matured in the twenty-five years since the early 1970s. Organizations like the Citizens Alliance for Public Planning and the Greenbelt Alliance served as resources for cities and towns contemplating their own slow-growth measures. Instead of starting from scratch, city councils and environmentalists could turn to organizations such as these for strategies and proposed ordinances.

Following on the heels of slow-growth measures in the 1970s and 1980s, the city of Santa Cruz adopted a greenbelt master plan stating, "The desire to maintain open space lands surrounding (as well as within) the City is an enduring concept. These lands help to define and protect the City's sense of place and environmental quality, and provide public safety, wildlife habitat and recreational opportunities" (City of Santa Cruz 1994, p. 5). The plan goes on to point out how greenbelt lands provide the town with open space buffers, "perceptible breaks in the urban fabric," and "a transition to lands in agricultural and grazing use." The plan repeatedly and explicitly cites as primary goals the inhibition of sprawl and concentration of urban development.

Language in the 1987 Santa Clara County Task Force report on open space was much stronger, beginning with a detailed account of urbanization patterns in the county since the 1950s. Indeed, the county had adopted an Urban Development/Open Space Policy Plan in 1973 that called for cities to confine their urban development to the areas within city boundaries. Noting that development policy was not being honored, the task force report went on to document what has now become familiar throughout the state: annexations permitted by the Local Agency Formation Commission, subdivisions of large parcels through certificates of compliance (a kind of automatic development approval), and private general plan amendments (a euphemism for variances granted by county supervisors).

The picture that emerges from the task force's short disquisition on land use regulation in Santa Clara County is one of mild resistance to formidable development pressure. It is not surprising, then, to find the task force calling not only for stronger enforcement of land use regulations but also for aggressive acquisition of land and easements. The 1987 task force's report identified as a priority the preservation of hundreds of thousands of acres for parks and open space, assigning highest importance to open space and farmland in or near riparian areas and under heavy development pressure. In 1999, local actors would add to the county's totals about 15,000 acres of open space, many of them in areas explicitly identified by the task force. The task force was itself a product of the county's preexisting policy capacity, and its report contributed further to local preservation resources.

Voters grew increasingly restive in the 1990s. Citizen resentment at lax zoning and land use enforcement on the part of city councils and boards of supervisors reached an all-time high by 1998. Sacramento County's unsteady enforcement of urban boundaries, the result of its willingness to rezone land, is typical of a weak regulatory approach to containing sprawl. As one newspaper account states,

> In the east county some powerful players in Sacramento are banking on the idea that the [urban limit] line will eventually be moved. They have amassed huge land holdings outside the development zone in hopes it will eventually be rezoned from agricultural to residential. Peter Detwiler, a consultant to the state Senate's Local Government Committee, said that pattern of land speculation is typical in jurisdictions that have urban limit lines subject to change by a handful of local politicians rather than by popular vote. "A speculator looks at where an urban limit line is and figures out the market may undervalue land just outside that line," Detwiler explained. "The speculator then buys undervalued land and uses his political connections to change the general plan. The same land that was worth $2,000 an acre yesterday as grazing land may now be worth $40,000 or $50,000 an acre as land that may be developed. When you're dealing with that kind of financial incentive, developers will work very hard to change the plan." (Vellinga 1999)

Overall, the growth machine at the end of the twentieth century was steaming ahead, only momentarily diverted here and there by pockets of resistance. As Pincetl points out, "At the grass-roots level, there were many local efforts to control the local effects of state's growth. Because they were scattered, individual, and unsystematic, these efforts did little to shape or curb the momentum of growth in the state" (1999, p. 161).

Despite the overwhelming power of the growth machine, nongovernmental organizations, local governments, and voters managed to preserve surprisingly large tracts of open space. Many of the ranches and parcels targeted for acquisition in the San Francisco and Monterey Bay areas did eventually find their way into public or land trust ownership. By 1999, about 91,000 acres had been acquired by the East Bay Regional Parks District, quite a bit more than the 6,200 acres that the East Bay Municipal Utility District was offering for sale in 1935. As one commentator on the Olmsted-Hall report of 1930 put it: "The East Bay Regional Parks District in its physical manifestations has utterly outshone the imagination of its midwives; where they foresaw a few surplus watersheds becoming parks, in fact, most surplus watersheds have become parks; beaches have become parks; intensive recreation sites have been acquired; unique landscape features, historical sites, and rare plant associations are protected in preserves" (Luten 1984).

Similarly, of six properties totaling 1,554 acres that the city of Santa Cruz designated in the mid-1980s as its greenbelt, four were purchased outright with city and state funds by 1999. Only the two smaller properties remained in private hands in 2000 (these totaled 74 acres).

CHANGES IN PRESERVATION POLICY PATTERNS

During the boom-and-bust cycles of development and their attendant antigrowth revolts, four enduring changes emerged in California's open space protection activities. These include, first, changes in intergovernmental relations, on the one hand, and changes in the relations between government and civil society, on the other. Second, the ability of local government to raise necessary funds for land preservation has declined dramatically; some jurisdictions, however, have more consistently overcome the new fiscal and political hurdles than others. Third, land preservationists have had to change and broaden their appeal in order to mobilize the substantial support needed to assemble wide conservation coalitions. Finally, new fiscal scarcity and policy failures have prompted preservationists to change the kinds of policy approaches and tools local governments have available for preservation purposes. Their use of nonacquisition means of local protection has vastly increased the acreage under protection, albeit with mixed results.

Intergovernmental Relationships and the Role of Civil Society

The first of these changes reflects a shift in the predominant political and institutional arena of local open space preservation decisions, previously populated by state and federal actors and now by local and nongovernmental actors. Not surprisingly, as the leadership has shifted, there have been associated changes in the points of intervention as well as in access to the policy process. As mentioned earlier, local open space preservation was pursued historically in more of a top-down fashion than it is today: elites (in and out of government, but generally in leadership positions) and technocrats were mainly responsible for initiating open space preservation efforts, while implementation was left largely to regional and state managers. This is less the case today as the relationships between the local, regional, state, and federal governments have changed, as have the roles of nongovernmental organizations.

Typical of recent environmental policy patterns, nongovernmental organizations are much more important to land protection than in the past: they still serve traditional roles, such as in attempting to sensitize the public to open space preservation issues and in raising money, but increasingly they serve as brokers of acquisitions, principal funders, and land managers. They also cultivate mass support for open space preservation, especially on ballot propositions.[7]

In 1985, the Land Trust Exchange (later, the Land Trust Alliance, a national clearinghouse based in Washington, D.C.) counted 32 land trusts in California, with a combined annual operating budget of almost $1.3 million (Land Trust Exchange 1985).[8] By 1994, that figure had risen to 119 land trusts (Land Trust Alliance 1995). Their work is complemented by some 400 Coordinated Resource Management and Planning programs and well over 600 nongovernmental environmental organizations. According to the 1997 National Directory of Conservation Land Trusts and my own surveys, 125 land trusts in the state were responsible for protecting some 571,000 acres in California (Land Trust Alliance 1998). Their annual operating budgets, as of summer 1994, amounted to at least $9 million, and their collective membership stood at approximately 173,300.[9]

The Harbinger File, a directory of environmental organizations, lists another 121 nongovernmental, noneducational organizations reporting land preservation as a major focus of their activities (Harbinger Communications 1998). Seventy of these additional organizations are local chapters of state or national organizations, such as the Audubon Society, California League of Conservation Voters, California Native Plant Society, League of Women Voters, and Sierra Club. Taken together, approximately 240 organizations throughout the state pursue local land preservation, generally with the support of local members and funds. Land preservation organizations are not evenly distributed throughout the state, however. Fully half of these organizations are based in only eight of California's fifty-eight counties, although they do not always confine their activities to a single county.

Not surprisingly, the number of land preservation organizations in a county is reasonably well correlated with the acreage protected in that county (see chapter 3), although numbers alone do not account for all preservation activity. Some land trusts and nongovernmental organizations are clearly much more effective than others, differing in their fund-raising, networking, and political mobilization abilities.

In a related development, schools and civic organizations across the state have begun to participate in adopt-a-creek, -river, -beach, -watershed, -park, and -highway activities. These activities involve hundreds of volunteers of all ages, though especially school-age children, in a combination of maintenance (i.e., cleanup), restoration, and natural history education. Almost 6 percent of the respondents to my survey reported being active in these efforts, suggesting that about 1.4 million California adults are engaged in some kind of cleanup effort every year.[10] Adding in school-age children would boost that figure substantially.

Some nongovernmental organizations are organized primarily to raise revenues for governmental entities; two notable examples include the Peninsula Open Space Trust, which was established in large part to raise funds for and donate lands to the Midpeninsula Regional Open Space District just south of San Francisco, and the Anza-Borrego Foundation, established in 1967 to benefit the Anza-Borrego Desert State Park in San Diego County. The trust was established in 1977 to leverage the public resources of the open space district with private funds (which often rise to $10 million or more per year). The trust has been directly responsible for protecting over 40,000 acres, much of which has been turned over to the open space district.

As is sometimes the case with national parks or forests, public open space land may entirely surround land held privately. In the mid-1960s, the California Parks and Recreation Commission asked a small group of

San Diego County residents to help acquire private inholdings within park boundaries. Those residents formed the Anza-Borrego Committee of the Desert Protective Council, becoming a nonprofit corporation—the Anza-Borrego Foundation—in 1989. This foundation acquires land through donation or purchase from willing sellers. Once acquired, the lands are transferred to Anza-Borrego Desert State Park. Since 1967 the foundation has acquired 26,000 acres (half of that since 1983), approximately half its ultimate goal. Today the Anza-Borrego Foundation works to preserve not only inholdings but also land adjacent to the park, and even remote property that may be traded for land within the park.

Funding

State financing of local open space preservation tends to come from three sources: statewide bond acts placed on the ballot; programs and funds created by the legislature expressly for funding park acquisition, some of which are dedicated to local assistance; and general fund expenditures. All these sources were in decline or moribund in the 1990s.

In 1928, California voters overwhelmingly approved Proposition 4 (almost 74 percent were in favor), a bond act raising $6 million for park acquisition and maintenance. After Proposition 4, there followed another twenty statewide measures (all occurring after 1962) largely devoted to raising funds for parks and habitat lands acquisition. Of the twenty-one total measures, fourteen passed and seven were defeated (in 1962, 1980, 1990, and 1994). Equally important, no new park bonds with major funding passed in the decade between the late 1980s and the late 1990s, although California legislators came close to putting a $600 coastal protection and park bond on the ballot in 1998. In 1999, they succeeded in putting a $2.1 billion bond measure on the March 2000 ballot.

Failure to approve park bonds does not necessarily signal changing voter priorities. For instance, electoral support for finance measures tracks closely with confidence in the economy (see Bowler and Donovan 1994). This helps to explain the spectacular defeat of the $2 billion Proposition 180, a park bond on the ballot in 1994, a time when many Californians still felt mired in recession. Frequently enough, park bond proponents in the legislature fail to amass the required two-thirds supermajority for moving park bond acts to the ballot—despite their general popularity—as happened in 1998, when popular parks and coastal measures were tied to controversial school- and water-funding proposals. Furthermore, between 1978 and 2000, the state did not use the general fund to compensate for these failed ballot initiatives. Quite the contrary. The general fund paid for 53 percent of the budget for the state Department of Parks and Recreation (DPR) in fiscal year 1988–1990, but such funding declined as a proportion of the budget in 1995–1996, to 27 percent (California Governor's Office 1996). Moreover, the DPR's budget had declined steadily since the early 1980s, partly because of the 1990–1992 recession and partly because state funding priorities changed. For example, in its fiscal year 1993–1994, the state of California had shifted $2.6 million in property tax revenue from local government to public school districts, thereby especially affecting counties and special districts; these local governments depend more on property taxes than do cities (Cal DPR 1994, p. 87). Most important for local open space efforts, local assistance funds administered by the state DPR had dropped from a two-decade high point of $145 million in 1989–1990 to $8.4 million in 1993–1994. These figures reflected the state's fiscal struggles during the recession of the early 1990s; since 1994–1995, local assistance has crept back up to about $30 million per year.

The primary election of March 2000 brought a return of state funding: voters overwhelmingly passed Proposition 12 (63 percent in favor), known as the Safe Neighborhood Parks, Clean Water, Clean Air, and Coastal Protection Act. This $2.1 billion bond act, the first passed by voters since 1988, provided $824 million in local assistance for a variety of recreation and open space–related land acquisition and park maintenance.

During the state's fiscal retreat, federal largesse had all but dried up. One of the most important sources of federal funding for parkland acquisition had been the federal Land and Water Conservation Fund (LWCF). This fund, created in 1964, relies mostly on royalties from oil and gas leases on the Outer Continental Shelf. Allocations to California had declined precipitously since the early 1980s. The LWCF had taken in about $19 billion between 1964 and 1996, but only $8 billion had been used, nationally, for park and habitat acquisition. The all-time high occurred in 1977–1978, when Congress approved about $800 million per year for parks and national preserves; beginning in the early 1980s, Congress spent $100 to 300 million per year for parks and preserves (Rogers 1996c). Between 1965 and 1992, the LWCF funded 334 state-level projects in California, valued at about $100 million, and 944 local-level projects, valued at approximately $130 million (Cal DPR 1994, pp. 42–43). Although California received as much as $26 million from the fund in 1979, the state was allocated less than $5 million per year between 1986 and the late 1990s.

Congress used the unappropriated balances in the LWCF for deficit reduction; however, beginning with the 105th Congress, legislators signaled a new willingness to restore LWCF funds. Congress passed an Interior Department budget that included $699 million for the LWCF; this was not quite the victory for local efforts it seemed, however, since the entire sum was earmarked for maintenance of existing national parks and for partial acquisition of the Headwaters Forest in Northern California. In 1999, the LWCF was definitively restored as the budget for 2000 appropriated nearly all of the fund for land preservation activities around the country. In 2000, Congress signaled its intention to provide $300 million per year out of the fund for ten years, by taking the LWCF out of the annual cycle of budget negotiations (Borenstein 2000). Like the California state government, the federal government renewed its commitment to funding land acquisition at a time of budget surpluses, record economic growth, and consumer confidence.

New Policy Objectives

Open space preservation today is still heavily focused on recreation, but habitat conservation, agricultural land preservation, flood and erosion protection, and growth management are increasingly important components. For example, most of the current mission statements, general plans, and multiyear plans for parks and recreation special districts have adopted a wildlife- or habitat-management component. Many cities and counties have exercised their land use authority to adopt "special area zones" to demarcate sensitive habitat, riparian ecosystem protections, and greenbelts (open spaces) or greenlines (urban boundaries) surrounding dense urban zones. This was the case especially with Proposition 117, passed in 1990, which required about $30 million in fund transfers for wildlife and habitat protection.[11]

Similarly, open space leaders often hitch their vision to other important issues already on the political agenda. By connecting different issues to one another, leaders create new values "by altering the context in which an idea is evaluated" (Rochon 1998, p. 79). In recent years, urban environmentalists have successfully tied their land acquisition proposals to crime prevention and youth programs. Referring to the 1992 and 1996 park ballot measures in Los Angeles, a campaign organizer pointed out:

> They were both called [the] Los Angeles County Safe Neighborhood Parks Act. They both had very strong safety components and gang prevention components in them. And it was pretty much pitched that way, with a vari-

ety of different types of improvements and types of, not just park projects, but senior projects, gang prevention projects, beach protection projects that would occur if this measure were to be passed. So it was really a quality of life issue, and we really stressed the fact that there were a lot of individual projects in this measure, that there was something for every single city, and [that] individual communities were really going to see a benefit from this. And that was part of the original design. We really worked very, very hard to make sure that would, in fact, be the case.

Changing Approaches and Policy Tools

Full fee acquisition, that is, outright ownership of parcels, is the principal form of local open space preservation discussed thus far. There are other ways to protect land; each has its advantages and disadvantages. Table 2 summarizes these different approaches and notes their applicability. Generally, local governments facing large-scale open space and conservation problems involving multiple agencies and multiple landowners (usually during times of fiscal scarcity) have turned to compensatory regulation (restriction accompanied by financial reward) to secure land protection without imposing all of the costs on private landowners (Glickfeld et al. 1995). But compensatory regulation—for all of its promise to free some landowners from bearing the costs of environmental protection alone—can be administratively very difficult. Regulators must have access to sophisticated information about land uses and values, and must be willing and able to raise private or public revenues with which to compensate landowners.

While acquisition can be the surest way to remove a developable property from future threat, it is an expensive strategy. Currently, parks and open space authorities routinely pay $5,000 to $50,000 per acre for new acquisitions (Greenbelt Alliance 1992; MROSD 1995; Rogers 1996b). Many of the most desirable parcels are attractive but expensive precisely because they are close to rapidly expanding cities and towns (see figure 8).

Moreover, land acquisition and management costs have gone up tremendously, much faster than the growth of local parks and open space agency budgets (Cal DPR 1988, 1994; Press et al. 1996). As costs have soared, local governments and nongovernmental organizations have turned to other conservation options, including special-area zoning, transferable development rights (in which development options are shifted from one place to another), conservation easements (in which development rights are donated by landowners), and purchased develop-

TABLE 2. LOCAL OPEN SPACE PRESERVATION POLICY OPTIONS

Nonregulation	Regulation	Compensatory Regulation
Relatively simple to administer	General plan land use designations	Offers possible regulatory relief, increased public land acquisition revenues, compensation for affected landowners, and permanent conservation
Generally supported by the public	Politically controversial	Difficult to administer
		May require public or private funding

Fee Simple Acquisition	Zoning	Land or Fee Exactions
Lands acquired outright	Relatively simple to administer	Developer pays fees (to be used for land acquisition) or donates land in exchange for development permit
Imposes management costs on the landowner	Imposes costs of preservation on the landowner	Reactive tool: preservation occurs only after development is under way
Generally the most expensive strategy		

Purchased and Donated Development Rights	Special-Area Zoning	Transferable Development Credits
Landowner sells development rights or donates them as a conservation easement	Regulates development rights, as in sensitive habitat or riparian zone ordinances	Landowner (sender) of open space, habitat, or agricultural land voluntarily agrees to sell or transfer development credits to a landowner-developer (receiver) wishing to increase the density on a developable parcel; local government facilitates by allowing an increase in density on the receiving parcel in exchange for a perpetual conservation easement on the receiving parcel
Works best when underlying economic value remains after transfer of rights, as in the case of agricultural and forestlands	Imposes costs on private sector	
	Not stable; can be removed by rezoning	

Mitigation Banking and Tradable Conservation Credits

Banks

Public or private entity acquires and manages open space lands for preservation ahead of any need for development

The entity banks mitigation credits from setting aside these lands against future development projects that have great impact

Tradable Credits

Developers pay conservation credits in exchange for the right to develop

Landowners who voluntarily preserve their land receive credits

Credits are then freely tradable on the market

SOURCE: Adapted from Glickfeld et al. 1995.

Figure 8. The Deer Hollow Farm in Rancho San Antonio County Park, Santa Clara County, just minutes from the heart of Silicon Valley. Photo by Victor Schiffrin.

ment rights (Glickfeld et al. 1995; Wright 1994). Although these methods of conservation tend to be less expensive than outright purchase, they have their own limitations. Special-area zoning, for example, regulates development rights in order to promote a wide range of public interest goals, including protection of sensitive or riparian habitats, agricultural land preservation, erosion control, and watershed management, to name but a few. It is the most controversial of the alternatives to outright purchase, relying as it does on the private sector to bear the costs of preservation. Furthermore, a change in city councils or boards of supervisors can quickly undo these protections.

Negotiations over transferable development rights tend to go smoothly only if there are relatively abundant and uncontroversial sites to which to transfer development, which is not the situation with the many cases involving sensitive habitats (usually wetlands). Conservation easements can offer attractive deductions, but landowners are often reluctant to give up development rights in perpetuity (Wright 1994). Purchased development rights can thus be quite expensive, to the point of negating the potential savings of buying the rights separate from the land. In the cases of both conservation easements and purchased development rights, the transaction costs (time, energy, legal counsel) of negotiating agreements between landowners, conservation groups, and local governments can be quite high.

Nonetheless, the land trusts that proliferated around the state during the 1980s have provided precisely the sorts of resources needed to overcome the transaction costs of negotiating conservation easements and purchased development rights. One of the largest purchased development rights agreements in the nation was negotiated in 1996 by the Monterey County Board of Supervisors, the Big Sur Land Trust, and a landowner with a substantial coastal ranch.

The 3,550-acre El Sur Ranch, a working property that had long been grazed, straddled scenic Highway 1 south of Monterey and Carmel. Because of its location on the coast, the property was highly desirable for resort or large-home development, but it was also subject to onerous restrictions under California's Coastal Act. After several unsuccessful development attempts, El Sur's owner negotiated with the Big Sur Land Trust. Although these discussions never bore fruit, the rancher had grown comfortable with the land trust. Thus, when Monterey County approached the ranch owner in 1997, he enlisted the land trust as his representative in negotiating a complex development rights deal (Colangelo 2000).

Ultimately, the Monterey County Board of Supervisors used $11.5 million in state bond act funds, left over from the 1988 Proposition 70, to purchase the development rights to El Sur Ranch (Rogers 1996a). The county sought the development rights specifically to protect views of the Big Sur coast—no public access is allowed and the property owners still run cattle on the ranch's extensive grasslands.

∎ ∎ ∎

A century of planning, policy innovation, and political mobilization tells a story of severe and growing resource constraints at the local level. One might expect declining local open space preservation efforts, but this has not been the case. Instead, local determination to preserve land has left California better equipped to deal with the growth machine than ever before. There are sophisticated and prescient land use plans, numerous land preservation organizations, and a public generally supportive of growth limits and land acquisition. In short, local policy capacity in this issue area has grown—though it has become greater in some counties than others—even as preservation has become more costly.

However, the growth machine at the beginning of the twenty-first century is more formidable than ever, aided by tremendous economic expansion and taxpayer revolts. Taking into account public desire for open space, habitat, and other environmental needs, the land preservation enterprise is woefully underfunded, especially in relation to the growth machine. The next chapter explores the contemporary context for local open space preservation, focusing on the physical, fiscal, and administrative factors shaping and constraining protection efforts.

Physical, Fiscal, and Administrative Landscapes

Chapter 1 identified regional, temporal, demographic, and institutional patterns of open space preservation in California. These patterns reveal an unambiguous and substantial variation in the amount of open space protected. For example, urban counties protect more land than rural counties do, and coastal regions protect more land than Central Valley regions do. Chapter 3 examines the reasons for this variation. Using the policy capacity model introduced in chapter 1, I show how various constraints and resources, both internal and external to a community, determine the success of that community in protecting open space.

DEVELOPMENT PRESSURE

New urban development steadily converts prime agriculture land and open space throughout California every year. (See figure 9.) Even the San Francisco Bay Area, home to the most aggressive slow-growth policies and active land preservationists, stands to lose one-eighth of the region's current open space to development during the next few decades. If development proceeds as planned, by 2030 the region will have urbanized an additional amount of land equivalent to 50 percent of the current urbanized land in the Bay Area (Greenbelt Alliance 2000).

When local residents perceive that the drawbacks of rapid development erode rather than enhance their communities, many are moved to embrace slow-growth or preservation strategies. Local perceptions of

Figure 9. Development pressure just outside Rancho San Antonio County Park, Santa Clara County. Photo by Victor Schiffrin.

runaway sprawl and soaring land and housing costs critically affect the context for land preservation around the state. I expect increasing development pressure to help motivate land preservation and growth controls. If a community's policy capacity to address environmental challenges develops while land prices are still relatively low, substantial preservation is possible. The most preservation—in total acres—happens in those communities with mature land preservation institutions (such as parks and recreation agencies and land trusts) and knowledgeable, supportive voters.

Although it is common for Californians to complain about traffic congestion, the loss of open space, and housing costs, the aggregate data on new housing starts and soaring property values obscure the variation in development pressure residents experience from place to place. To give a picture of the development pressure around the state, I have chosen two indicators, each at the county aggregate level: the number of new housing units permitted between 1965 and 1998 and the change in assessed property valuation during that time (see figures 10 and 11).

Changes in property values are not felt as development pressure

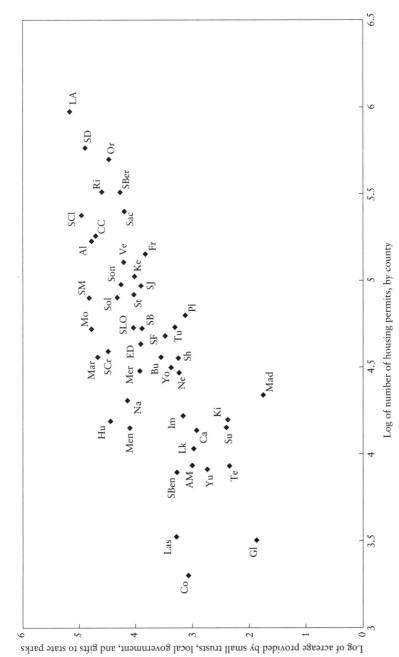

Figure 10. Relationship between number of new housing permits and land preservation, 1965–1996. (N = 47 counties, R = 0.73) A list of county abbreviations can be found on p. xi.

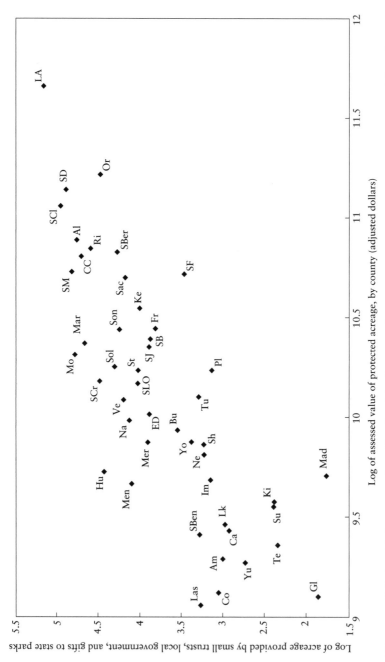

Figure 11. Relationship between value of land and land preservation, 1965–1998. (N = 47 counties, R = 0.79) A list of county abbreviations can be found on p. xi.

immediately; there is a lag time between the change in land prices and the conversion or abandonment of good agricultural land, on the one hand, and substantial increases in new infrastructure and building construction, on the other. Figures 10 and 11 suggest a robust relationship between development and land preservation. In both figures, Los Angeles, Orange, Santa Clara, and San Diego Counties lead in development and preservation; however, the sequence of development and preservation certainly differs in each place. Los Angeles County has many acres preserved, but relatively few per capita. As the state's "super-county," Los Angeles has drawn on a formidable tax base since 1950 to acquire land, but the county developed too rapidly for preservation to keep pace with the rate in other counties around the state, much less for preservation to keep pace with the acres eaten up by sprawl within the county itself.

Perceptions of development also vary throughout the state. In my "Community and Conservation in California Survey" conducted during 1997 and 1998 (see appendix 2), 18 percent of all respondents statewide agreed that "development of hillsides, wetlands, or other natural areas" was a problem in their community; 15 percent felt that the loss of family farms was a problem where they lived. The picture is quite different when viewed from a local perspective. For example, only 7 percent of respondents in the southern San Joaquin Valley felt that development was a problem, whereas about a quarter of Amador County respondents replied that it was a problem in their county. The range of replies pinpointing farm loss as a problem is even greater, from just under 6 percent in San Francisco County (which has had no significant farm acreage in decades) to over 25 percent in Amador County. A few years after this survey was conducted, another survey, by the Public Policy Institute of California, also found wide variation in perceptions of development pressure. In that survey, 47 percent of San Francisco Bay Area respondents felt that population growth and development were a big problem in their region, while only 21–27 percent felt the same way in Los Angeles and other parts of Southern California. Of Central Valley respondents, only 17 percent felt growth was a big problem (PPIC 2000). The development indicators and survey data make it clear that development pressure varies from county to county, that people are attuned to this variation, at least in the sense that they view it differently from county to county, and thus that the fact of development pressure and its variation *and* the perception of pressure make sense as motivators of land preservation.

There are several ways in which development pressure contributes to local open space preservation. First, urban sprawl is hard to ignore; it thus serves as a psychological spur to land acquisition. A common plea heard around California states the need to prevent one's region from "becoming another Los Angeles."

When asked why voters in the small Sonoma County town of Windsor passed an urban growth boundary in 1996, a city council member replied:

> I heard this over and over. A lot of them had moved up here from L.A. or San Jose and didn't want to live like that any more. . . . The county was sending . . . all the housing up here; . . . the schools were behind, we have portable schools; we had road traffic, . . . you know, inadequate roads; the parks were way behind; we weren't getting any of the infrastructure, we were just getting the housing—a thousand a year.

Development is particularly noticeable in the coastal foothill counties, where valleys are narrow enough to show dramatic land use changes. Park and open space district managers frequently cite the visual impact of urban sprawl as a powerful motivator of growth management (see figure 12). Indeed, the enabling legislation of the Santa Clara Open Space Authority, established in 1992, recommends that "priority for open-space acquisition should be focused on those lands closest, most accessible, and *visible* to the urban area" (emphasis added).[1] Whether urban sprawl must be visible to most people in a community in order to effectively prompt support for open space preservation is unclear; certainly many valley counties with flatter topographies preserve open space, though typically these surround rivers, lakes, and reservoirs.

A second, related, way in which development encourages local open space preservation is by prompting demand for recreation accessible to urban and suburban centers. As sprawl progresses, the average travel time to open space increases, particularly if mass transit serves only a few major corridors. For years, city and county planners, local legislators, and local parks officials have attempted to maintain open space access in ratios ranging from at least two acres per thousand residents to fifteen acres per thousand residents (Nelson 1988; USORRRC 1962). These ratios are considered essential, especially for passive recreation such as hiking or camping.

Third, and less directly tied to development, different patterns of land ownership hinder or permit open space acquisitions. Eric Jessen, an official with Orange County's special Harbors, Beaches and Parks District, explains how the pattern created by a legacy of large landholdings has contributed to the success of open space protection in Orange County.

Figure 12. Heavy equipment for a large development in Contra Costa County. Photo by Richard J. Meisinger Jr.

According to Jessen, much of Orange County had been held in large estates by three families, whose lands had derived from the legacy of the great land holdings that had produced the original Spanish ranchos and haciendas. The Bixbys, in the northern part of the county, had owned a vast tract of land known as Rancho Los Alamitos. In the middle part of the county, the Irvine Ranch had been created from Rancho San Joaquin and Rancho Santa Ana, previously owned by the Sepulvedas and the Yorbas, respectively. And in the southern part of the county, the O'Neill family had acquired the huge Rancho Santa Margarita y Los Flores. This legacy has left large blocks of real estate ownership intact. "The O'Neills still own about 40,000 acres, the Irvine Company owns about 80,000. . . . Generally speaking, Orange County has a high incidence of 500–5000 acre parcels." The significance of these large parcels, explains Jessen, is that "when developers have that amount of land to work with, they need to cluster their development to keep their infrastructure costs down . . . and, consistent with county policy, this maximizes the amount of land that can be set aside for open space." He emphasizes that planners can "play around with developers who have this kind of land because you're not putting an unfair financial burden on them[,] . . . not like the guy with five acres who can't afford to give up a square inch."

By comparison, most other California counties were not held in such large parcels originally. For example, to this day, San Diego County farm sizes are considerably smaller than those in Orange County (US DOA 2002). It is more difficult to protect smaller exurban parcels. They are generally less important as ecological habitat or as growth boundaries, in part because it is so difficult to stitch together large, contiguous parcels from small fragmented ones.

Finally, development increases the level of fiscal resources available to local government, some of which may be relatively "loose," or uncommitted, funds. Uncommitted funds are discretionary resources remaining after mandatory expenditures for schools and certain kinds of infrastructure are made. Describing how the Orange County Board of Supervisors welcomed development as long as it paid its way, a planning veteran remarked that the board of supervisors "adopted a policy that said that the regional parks system will emerge as a result of urbanization, and not despite it. That's a euphemism for saying, 'We're going to extract these lands from developers at no cost.'" To the extent that they raise property and sales tax revenues, the construction and real estate industries play roles not only as the engines of development but also as (willing or unwilling) partners in preservation. Developers know that land values increase with proximity to protected open space and thus are sometimes amenable to voluntarily mitigating their projects by setting portions of their lands aside. Since the passage of the 1965 Quimby Act, California cities and counties have been authorized to pass ordinances requiring that developers either set aside land or pay fees for park dedications. These "development impact fees" can become quite substantial; the fees are not reported to the state but appear only in city and county budgets and, unfortunately, data about them are not readily accessible. The surveys that have been conducted estimate that cities and counties in 1981 assessed an average of $800 per dwelling unit in park dedication fees.[2] As of 1996, 268 cities and thirty counties had passed Quimby Act ordinances (California Governor's Office of Planning and Research 1999).

These jurisdictions issued permits for well over 90,000 new, privately owned housing units in 1994 (California Department of Finance 1998). If only 50,000 of these 90,000 permits raised an average of $1,000 in park dedication fees, the total amassed for acquisition and maintenance would be $50 million—more than the combined budgets of local land trusts and certainly on a par with the local assistance grants currently being administered by the state Department of Parks and Recreation.[3] Thus, by the measure of park dedication fees alone, development and urbanization in California provide a substantial portion of the total public funds available for park and open space acquisition and maintenance.

But the distribution of these funds is skewed. According to the *California Planners' Book of Lists,* issued annually by the California Governor's Office of Research, 119 of the 208 jurisdictions in Southern California have adopted a Quimby Act ordinance. My research assistants and I conducted a mail survey of Quimby Act ordinances for this book. Among those responding to our survey, the range of fees varied but was difficult to compare because of differing permit-fee formulas. A number of jurisdictions have a flat per-unit fee for single-family dwellings and a sliding fee for multifamily dwellings. These all range from $800 to $3,000 per unit. Beyond these two means of calculation, there is even greater variation: the city of Los Angeles, for instance, has a fee formula based on the value of land being developed, which varies according to zone and number of units, so the fee amount changes. In nearby Palos Verdes Estates, developers must dedicate for park purposes an area equal to 50 percent of the total area of lots to be used for private purposes in the subdivision.

A better comparison can be made of the total amount of money collected. In 1996, revenue generated ranged from a low of $4,396 in Downey to a high of $2,550,000 in the rapidly urbanizing city of San Marcos. This shows how development fees can favor rapidly urbanizing suburban areas without benefiting inner city areas. As an open space ballot organizer in Los Angeles put it:

> [The] Quimby Act provides almost nothing, just a tiny drop in the bucket; and because [of] the circle or the distance that [the] Quimby Act draws around development, unfortunately the majority of those developments that have generated any kind of real Quimby money have not been in those areas which are in most dire need. . . . [New developments] tend to be in higher income areas, . . . so the Quimby money generally gets spent on some kind of park development project. . . . I can't think of a single park or piece of land that has been bought with Quimby. And the land values in the city are quite high, even in what people consider less desirable areas they are very high. . . . [A] whole other subject of needs is revising Quimby to be more meaningful today than it was when it was written.

Only three entities reported accepting land in 1996, nothing totaling more than 100 acres—which may indicate that governments are obtaining parklands from mechanisms other than Quimby Act ordinances.

Development pressure is a complex bundle of effects, some psychological or perceptual and others more material. A perception of development pressure is almost certainly a necessary but not sufficient precondition for land preservation. In some parts of the state, communities respond to development pressure with successful campaigns to block new construction or to acquire sensitive lands. The little coastal town of Santa Cruz resisted ranchette-style development on the Bombay property—a 240-acre parcel with ravines, pasture, and ocean views on the city's western edge—for a decade before voters approved a bond measure to acquire the property in 1998.

In many other communities, such as Fair Oaks in Sacramento County, residents succeed only in shrinking proposed developments. The proposed Gum Ranch development in Fair Oaks started out as a plan to build six hundred homes and a 17-acre shopping center on 107 acres of farmland (Yost 1995). Two years later, the developer had scrapped over half of the planned homes and proposed setting aside open space in lieu of building the shopping center (Yost 1997).

In sum, overdeveloped communities that cannot mount successful preservation campaigns share some or all of the following three characteristics:

· they grow too rapidly to manage development, say, through the mobilization of a slow- or antigrowth constituency and leadership;

· land prices outstrip the funding capacity of land preservation organizations;

· very few relatively large parcels close to urban areas are available for acquisition.

Los Angeles County is the most obvious example of a part of the state where political support for containing growth and acquiring land has been "too little and too late."

THE PRESERVATION OF SPECIAL LANDSCAPES

If the specter of sprawl is a powerful motivator of preservation, so are the state's compelling foothills and river valleys. In our discussions around the state, local government officials and private conservationists alike frequently commented on the importance of maintaining open vistas on hillsides and access to scenic rivers. In addition to acting out of aesthetic concern, communities set aside special landscapes to protect against erosion, hilltop wildfires, and river channelization and other forms of riparian habitat degradation.[4]

Figure 13. The American River Parkway in Sacramento during summer, far below the levee. Photo by Daniel Press.

Rivers

Establishing a river parkway is an especially attractive way to preserve land in the state's flat Central Valley and in areas where other county lands are unavailable for purchase (see figure 13). Members of environmental organizations support acquisitions of riparian corridors because of the environmental amenities and habitat connectivity they bring, while most other residents are likely to be motivated by recreational and aesthetic concerns (Kline and Wichelns 1998).

As in partnerships formed strictly for land preservation, private land trusts and local governments commonly work together for riparian protection. The San Joaquin River Parkway Trust was established in the late 1980s by Fresno County residents concerned about access to the San Joaquin and protection of its banks. Trust members spent half a decade mobilizing two dozen local governments and nongovernmental organizations on behalf of the river. Eventually, Fresno's assemblymember Jim Costa led the effort to create the San Joaquin River Conservancy, a state agency spanning the multiple county and city lines crossed by the San Joaquin. Advocates pushed for a *state* conservancy, rather than a regional special district, because they could then count on the parkway's acquisition, operation, and maintenance costs having a permanent place in the state budget (Koehler 2000).

San Diego County provides another example of riparian protection. The San Dieguito River Valley Regional Open Space Park grew out of a joint powers authority made up of San Diego County and the cities bordering the San Dieguito River on its way from four-thousand-foot Volcan Mountain to the ocean at Del Mar, some fifty-five miles away. As Diane Coombs, executive director of the San Dieguito River Park Joint Powers Authority, put it, widespread involvement led to the park's formation:

> It was people in the San Dieguito planning group, people in Del Mar, people in Rancho Santa Fe and [the] League of Women Voters . . . who were saying, "This is our last remaining river valley and we need to protect it." And they began pressuring government. Government followed public opinion; it did not lead. And the city of San Diego hired consultants to do some plans for the city lands in the river valley. And then the county did a sort of a concept plan for the county lands in the river valley.

Coombs went on to note that the Joint Powers Authority also enjoys broad-based assistance in its region:

> The [San Dieguito] River Valley Land Conservancy and several of the people I mentioned earlier are involved in [volunteer activity]. That's a support organization. And we have a citizens advisory committee that is composed of approximately forty organizations. So we have representations from environmental organizations, we have property-owner representatives, we have community planning group representatives, we have neighborhood association representatives, professional association representatives; and they meet generally monthly.

If river corridors compel significant land acquisitions, then we should see a positive relationship between local land preservation and the presence of major rivers in a given county. Moreover, local governments and land trusts operating in or near the urban fringe would be more likely to create river parks in close proximity to cities and towns rather than in remote rural areas (see figure 14).

To determine whether this was the case, I used a geographic information systems (GIS) map overlaying major rivers inside county boundaries with the 1990 census designations of urban and rural tracts.[5] This overlay permitted me to isolate urban rivers from rural ones and, in

Figure 14. Coyote Creek, a river parkway east of San Jose, in Santa Clara County. Photo by Victor Schiffrin.

effect, to see whether counties with major waterways were more likely to engage in land preservation activities. Figure 15 shows that local preservation is indeed associated with the number of miles traced by major rivers within the urbanized parts of California counties. This result is not surprising, given that urban rivers in California are often associated with attractive, often hilly, landscapes, on which development pressure is easily noticed.

Hillsides

California's busy geology endowed the state not only with the spectacular peaks of the Sierra Nevada but also with several coastal foothill ranges. These gentler hillsides bound many urban areas, presenting compelling vistas—and hence attracting development—but also problems. Many of the state's residents have visceral reactions to the idea of building on the remaining hills covered by oak woodlands, chaparral, or redwoods. Several municipalities around the state restrict construction on behalf of "viewsheds" and have acquired dozens of conservation ease-

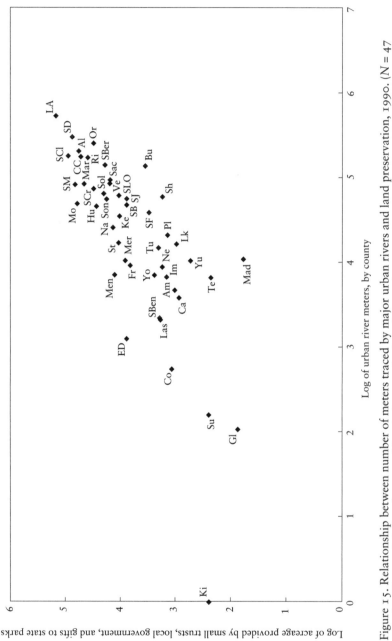

Figure 15. Relationship between number of meters traced by major urban rivers and land preservation, 1990. (N = 47 counties, R = 0.74) A list of county abbreviations can be found on p. xi.

ments specifically to protect the open vistas afforded by unencumbered hills in the exurban zone.

Hillsides offer many residents an appealing variety in their landscapes. One park planner in Monterey County pointed out that residents of the Salinas Valley want open space on the surrounding hillsides: "For people who live in a flat land that's very windy, what would be the primary source of recreation for them? Different topography, different geography—it would be the foothills, of course. So you create foothill parks for these flatland cities. They're close, you can go to them directly." A Marin County park acquisitions director stressed the local significance of preserving foothills: "While we have not had any success with the countywide [park ballot] measure, we've had very, very good success with local measures to protect open space. And the motivation is primarily [that] people don't want to be looking at a new development on that hillside."

Other pragmatic and economic motives contribute to restrictions on hillside construction. It is expensive to provide infrastructure such as roads, sewers, water, and power on steeper grades, and equally difficult to pay for services such as police and fire protection, schools, and sanitation. Moreover, several coastal counties have watched prime agricultural land converted to development; elsewhere, foothills with important oak woodlands or chaparral have been planted to vineyards. Thus, the net total of agricultural acres may not change much, but the location of farming and recreation is nonetheless seriously impacted.

Accordingly, many land trusts and local governments are specifically mandated by their charters or enabling legislation to keep development off the hills. Many of the crown jewels of the state's land trusts or regional recreation or open space districts consist of large hillside ranches; good examples include the holdings of the East Bay Regional Parks District, the Midpeninsula Regional Open Space District, and the several agencies preserving open space in Southern California's Santa Monica Mountains.

As in the case of rivers, if hillsides compel significant land acquisitions, then we should see a positive relationship between local land preservation and hillier counties. And, local governments and land trusts operating in or near the urban fringe would be more likely than those in remote rural areas to protect nearby hilly areas and open spaces (see figure 16).

To measure the effect of hillsides on preservation, I used a GIS map overlaying the mean elevation of ninety-square-meter points for all forty-seven study counties, and the 1990 census designations of urban and rural tracts.[6] Reasoning that a county's many elevation points would

Figure 16. The Bombay property, Santa Cruz. This greenbelt preserve is cut by a deep gorge and creek. Photo by Victor Schiffrin.

have greater *variability* in a hillier rather than a flatter urban zone, I used the standard deviation of each county's ninety-square-meter elevation data points.[7] Correlating elevation with the number of protected acres yielded an R of 0.34, which suggests that local preservation is somewhat related to the standard deviation of elevation in the urbanized parts of California counties.

FISCAL RESOURCES

It is reasonable to assume that wealthier communities are better able and more likely to spend scarce private resources and tax dollars on open space. Indeed, it makes sense that wealthier people might more energetically support land acquisition and zoning regulations to maintain the vistas that make their communities desirable and keep property values high and rising. Similarly, wealthy communities might use open space preservation as a way of gating their communities and buffering them from sprawl and lower-income development.

Chapter 2 described the devastating fiscal effect of antitax measures; however, some counties, including Alameda, Contra Costa, Orange, and Santa Clara, enjoy the benefits of relatively "antitax proof" institutions whose taxation powers predate Proposition 13 by many years. One Orange County planner extolled the fiscal strength of the state's older, large special recreation and parks districts:

> The fundamental key is this concept of a countywide special district, or in the case of the East Bay, a two-county special district, that gives you a strong financial base. And when you have property tax revenues that are accumulating in the bank, and you've got concession revenue accumulating in the bank, and you're parking grant revenues in the bank, you're also earning interest, which is another major source of revenue. For years, our system was growing so fast that we couldn't get the projects built fast enough, which meant that the money stayed in the bank longer.

A Monterey County parks planner echoed this sentiment, adding that city and county governments must balance competing uses for local revenues and are therefore not likely to focus their funding as consistently on land acquisition: "Cities have a multiple role to play[;] . . . we have one role. We're a single purpose district, [and our purpose is] to buy and preserve, acquire open space. [The cities' roles . . . and purposes] change."

Unfortunately, directly measuring the relationship between wealth and preservation is difficult, mainly because lands are acquired over several decades, but wealth is usually measured only annually. The ideal way of measuring the relationship between wealth and acquisitions within a community would be to correlate both in a continuous time series. Such data are not available, primarily because dates for land acquisition more than five or ten years in the past are exceedingly difficult to reconstruct.

But economic resources are surely an important factor for any local government program. As a regional open space district staffer pointed out, "You can't have open space without the commerce to support it." For the purpose of exploring the relationship between wealth and acquisition, I totaled the local government revenues from cities, counties, and special districts for the period 1965 to 1996 (the period during which most local land acquisitions occurred; figures are adjusted to 1995 dollars), aggregated at the county level. I chose local government receipts for several reasons. First, government revenues are a more sensible measure of the community wealth available for public goods such as parks and greenbelts than per capita income. Per capita income is an unreliable indicator because the wealthiest communities may prefer to secure environmental goods privately, say through private golf courses or other green spaces in gated communities, through leisure travel, or by acquiring large estates. Second, government receipts comprehensively account not only for the importance of local economies but also for local voters' willingness to approve public funding measures at the ballot box. Third, local government revenues are measures of the total fiscal potential in a given county. These figures reveal nothing of how funds were spent, but indicate only that certain funds were available for the wide variety of public purposes and mandates characteristic of local government.

The residential tax base could also be used to explore the wealth thesis, since many special districts rely on property tax assessments for revenues. However, most city and county parks and open space agencies do not rely on property tax assessments, thus I have not measured the residential property tax base against local acreage acquisitions.

In short, valuable land on California's urban fringe is very expensive. Moreover, the important open space acres still available for protection in wealthier communities are almost always more expensive than land on the urban fringe in communities with more modest means. While it makes sense that communities with greater relative spending power should be able to acquire more land for preservation (see figure 17), that fiscal strength is tempered by California's skyrocketing land prices.

As strong as the relationship portrayed in figure 17 may be, it is only somewhat illuminating. The effect that general local government revenue might have on a particular local public expenditure is problematic in the same way Putnam found it to be in the relationship between economic modernity and provincial government performance in Italy:

> Economic modernity is somehow associated with high-performance public institutions—that much is clear. What our simple analysis cannot reveal is whether modernity is a cause of performance (perhaps one among several), whether performance is perhaps in some way a cause of modernity, whether both are influenced by a third factor (so that the association between the two is in some sense spurious), or whether the link between modernity and performance is even more complex. (1993, p. 86)

As was the case with development pressure, we should view fiscal resources as a necessary condition for land preservation, but not a sufficient one. Wealthier communities could plausibly opt out of providing

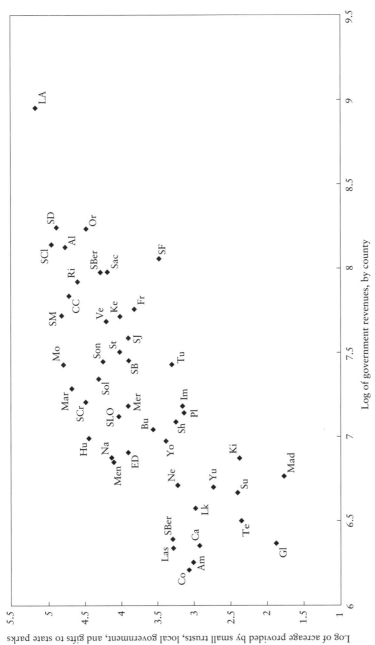

Figure 17. Relationship between government revenues and land preservation, 1965–1996. (N = 47 counties, R = 0.75) A list of county abbreviations can be found on p. xi.

public environmental goods. They could also lack the political will and administrative expertise to commit a portion of even relatively abundant resources to land preservation.

ADMINISTRATIVE RESOURCES

Cities and counties in California also vary in their administrative abilities. Some have large planning staffs with specialized expertise; others have access to sophisticated geographic information systems providing valuable information about city and county land uses.[8] Not surprisingly, the larger jurisdictions have larger planning staffs. Smaller, less affluent communities tend to have smaller and less well-trained staffs, what one planner pejoratively called "seat-of-the-pants employees." For example, tiny Alpine County (1993 population of 1,200) reported having one planner for the entire county in 2001. The county of Los Angeles and its cities reported having more than five hundred planners in 2001, or one planner for approximately every 17,000 residents (California Governor's Office of Planning and Research 1999). Of course, the numbers alone do not indicate whether Alpine County can complete its planning tasks as well as or better than Los Angeles County. Differences in staff numbers are to be expected, but having a larger staff might enable a county to plan more effectively for the particular lands and land uses involved and may also permit specialization.

Local agencies develop long-standing expertise that can be (but certainly is not always) marshaled in service of land preservation. For example, officials at the state Department of Parks and Recreation pointed out that they have come to expect timely, compelling, and comprehensive grant proposals from the East Bay Regional Parks District, which spans portions of Alameda and Contra Costa Counties alongside San Francisco Bay (Verardo 1997). And indeed, the parks district raised just under $7 million in competitive grants between 1964 and 1996, second only to the $8.5 million raised by the county of Los Angeles.

Jurisdictions that have relatively large planning staffs can assign some grant-writing positions and thereby take advantage of external (usually intergovernmental) funding sources. Other administrative abilities might consist of expertise in information technologies, land use and real estate law, biological assessment, campaign management (especially of public finance initiatives submitted to local electorates), and finance. Each of these capabilities can assist a local government in identifying and acting on land preservation opportunities.

The Santa Clara County parks department hired specialists in real estate appraisals and transactions. I asked one of these specialists if this indicated a high volume of land acquisition by the parks agency, and was told:

> I think it was quite apparent, when I got hired, that that was the case, because though they had the funds accumulated . . . the existing staff in the county, as a whole, wasn't adequate to mount a concerted effort to acquire parkland. There were good professional people who were providing services to the department for acquisition and leasing and other property rights matters that go on that people seldom really are aware of.

To convey the importance of administrative capacity with quantitative data, I constructed an index consisting of the following:

· Log of competitive park grants made to city, county, special recreation, and parks districts by county, for 1964 to 1995 (Martin 1998)
· Planners per county in 1994 (California Governor's Office of Planning and Research 1995)
· Number of jurisdictions per county that had GIS in 1995 (California Governor's Office of Planning and Research 1996)
· Number of jurisdictions that had training programs for their planning commissions in 1998 (California Governor's Office of Planning and Research 1999)

The first measure in the index consists of the sum of competitive grants awarded by the state Department of Parks and Recreation and the federal Land and Water Conservation Fund. Just under $80 million (unadjusted) was granted to cities, special districts, and counties for land acquisitions between 1964 and 1996. Jurisdictions competed for these funds; they were not block allocations. Larger jurisdictions certainly raised more funds than smaller ones; however, population size alone is not a good indicator of a county's ability to raise such revenues.

The Governor's Office of Research collected data on the remaining measures in its annual surveys for the *California Planners' Book of Lists;* each variable measures a county's professional competence in land use planning and policy implementation. Table 3 shows that the four measures are well intercorrelated.

Figure 18 shows the relationship between administrative capacity and open space preservation in the forty-seven-county data set. Administra-

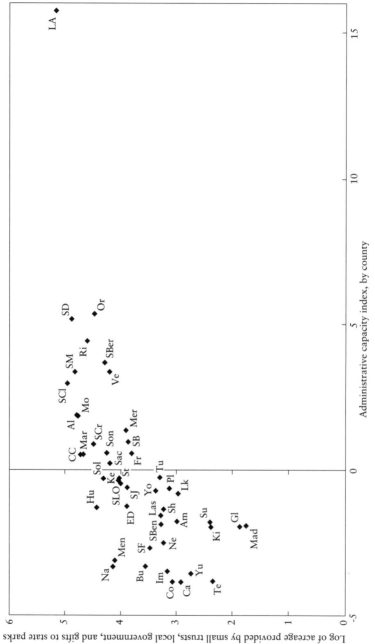

Figure 18. Relationship between administrative capacity and land preservation, 2000. ($N = 47$ counties, $R = 0.65$) A list of county abbreviations can be found on p. xi.

TABLE 3. ADMINISTRATIVE CAPACITY
INTERCORRELATIONS

	Planners per county	Park grants raised per county	Planning commission training, by county	Jurisdictions using GIS
Planners per county	1.000			
Park grants raised per county	0.363	1.000		
Planning commission training, by county	0.839	0.440	1.000	
Jurisdictions using GIS	0.676	0.460	0.806	1.000

SOURCES: California Governor's Office of Planning and Research 1999; Martin 1998.
NOTE: N = 47 counties.

tive capacity is associated with preservation nearly to the same degree as development pressure or fiscal resources.

• • •

To local political leaders, development pressure, landscape features, and fiscal and administrative resources all appear to be exogenous factors they must manipulate, mitigate, enhance, or leverage in the attempt to slow growth or preserve land. None of these contextual factors changes quickly or easily as a result of local efforts. State policy and economic cycles more rapidly and profoundly affect local finances than do local government efforts to stimulate revenues. Similarly, local leaders change development patterns over a period of decades, but rarely with more than city-level effects.

What communities and their leaders make of these factors determines whether growth is contained and land preserved, *at the margin*. Chapter 4 turns to the civic context for land preservation, showing that communities in California differ greatly with respect to their expectations about collective environmental goods as well as their efforts at securing local environmental protection.

CHAPTER 4

Civic and Environmental Voluntarism in California

Civic activities on behalf of environmental protection in California have a long history. As early as 1868, San Diego's Balboa Park, a 1,200-acre open space within the city, enjoyed widespread support from civic and women's groups. In 1870, a petition of 353 signers went to the state legislature asking it to confirm the action of the city trustees in setting aside the park. The leaders of the petition drive included key city founders such as Alonzo Horton. Letters in the archives of the city of San Diego include an 1889 petition by "the Ladies Auxiliary of the Chamber of Commerce" to adopt 10 acres of the park and improve them. Similar requests from the Women's Civic Improvement Society of San Diego and the "improvement clubs" of the neighborhoods of Middletown, Southern View, Arlington-Nordica, Imperial Heights, and Ocean View stretch into the 1920s. Support for parks, and for Balboa Park in particular, was at such a level that various citizens of the town, including the San Diego Hotel Men's Association, requested that residents be taxed by the city and funds be given to the parks department for improvements.

Similarly, the extensive state parks holdings in the Santa Cruz Mountains enjoyed concerted efforts by local civic improvement groups. Their leadership founded the Sempervirens Club (later the Sempervirens Fund) in 1900 with the purpose of acquiring old-growth redwoods in San Mateo, Santa Clara, and Santa Cruz Counties. Contemporary activists would recognize in the club's strategies many of the same efforts used today: lobbying the state legislature and governor for state funds, petition drives, tours for potential donors and political allies to the proposed park sites, photographic displays at expositions in major cities, and editorials in local and regional dailies. Even the call to action "Save the trees!" dates back to 1900, published in a letter to the *Santa Cruz Sentinel* by Josephine McCrackin (Yaryan 1999).

One commentator in Marin reflected on the combination of geographic isolation and civic engagement contributing to that county's early and sustained commitment to open space preservation: "Prior to 1937 there were people that had the insight to know, to recognize that construction of the Golden Gate Bridge was going to change Marin County. And at that time the Marin Conservation League was formed, which has been instrumental in preserving and protecting Marin County through the years."

As the policy capacity model suggests, a strongly engaged community can sometimes achieve its goals with relatively few of the other capacity factors present (especially if fiscal resources are lacking). The extensive greenbelt around the coastal city of Santa Cruz is a case in point. Santa Cruz began the 1970s not particularly wealthy, relative to other counties, nor was it led by pro-preservation council members or supervisors. Many community members, however, were deeply concerned about development proposals for the remaining open space on the city's waterfront and for farmland and forest on the city's western edge.

In the mid-1970s, activists largely outside of local government began mobilizing on behalf of a greenbelt vision. The idea was to encircle the city with open space, first by actually naming parcels the activists wanted included, then by figuring out later how to protect them. One of the prize parcels was a 614-acre lot called Pogonip that abutted the University of California and boasted mixed redwood forest and oak woodlands with spectacular ocean views. Though it was held privately, Pogonip was heavily used by city residents and university students (see figure 19). Open space advocates put Measure O on the ballot in 1979, which imposed a ten-year development moratorium on designated greenbelt land, including the popular Pogonip property and a 246-acre ranch on the western edge of town owned by the Bombay Corporation. Measure O passed with overwhelming support. As a then member of the Santa Cruz City Council put it, the campaign "ended up being a fairly broad movement of different people. Most, almost all of the rallies that took place . . . focused mainly on the Pogonip, slow growth." Owners of greenbelt lands sued the city, arguing that Measure O constituted a fifth-amendment taking (unlawful government seizure without just compensation). However, they lost their

Figure 19. A jogger in Pogonip, a heavily used city park in Santa Cruz that also harbors important plant and animal communities. Photo by Victor Schiffrin.

case, largely because the city had always been willing to permit agricultural activities and other low-impact land uses and thus had never deprived the landowners of all the properties' value.

For the remainder of the 1970s and 1980s, the city did not pay for the greenbelt parcels it protected; instead, very energetic civic activity spurred new city councils and county supervisors to work with the state and private organizations to provide funds for some of the key initial purchases. A major victory occurred in 1988, when the statewide California Parks and Wildlife Initiative (Proposition 70) passed. The campaign for Proposition 70 was led by the Sacramento-based Planning and Conservation League, but it sought help from volunteers throughout the state. In return for this promised help, the league wrote specific properties and their costs into the initiative, based on how much a county's residents worked on the campaign. A Santa Cruz City Council member who had been active in the campaign noted that the $15 million Pogonip parcel was the prize promised to the country in exchange for local efforts mounted on behalf of Proposition 70:

> We were active in [the Proposition 70 campaign], and we got [Pogonip] designated as one of the properties that the city would use. . . . You [had]

some input in terms of how much money you [received]. . . . [It] wasn't the city formally, but the city residents, and activists here, the Sierra Club and others' willingness to work on this issue, to push it, help provide signatures. We gathered our share of signatures, which had some impact on it, and the result was that we got a bigger chunk than the smallest county in California likely would have got, because of the political activism we had around the issue.

By the mid- to late 1990s, city leadership and experience with slow growth and land preservation had matured. The city used its general fund to purchase another segment of its greenbelt, the expensive but highly prized 40-acre Arana Gulch property. A few years later, the city was able to buy the Bombay property following a skillfully organized ballot campaign for a measure that was ultimately approved by 71 percent, a comfortable margin above the required two-thirds. What had been unthinkable or very difficult twenty years earlier—general fund purchases or supermajority approvals for local bonds—had been carefully and deliberately brought into the realm of the possible. In effect, the community first *compensated* for its lack of several policy capacity elements—fiscal and administrative resources—then went on in subsequent years to *develop* these relatively absent factors.

Repeated examples of such civic voluntarism in many different policy arenas have brought on new interest in concepts of political culture, particularly as they relate to public policy outputs and outcomes (Almond 1997; Inglehart 1988). Recent contributions include works relating political-cultural or civic culture factors to economic growth and government performance or social unrest (Granato et al. 1996; Inglehart 1988; Putnam 1993; Varshney 1998). Following on Coleman's 1988 article proposing the term "social capital" and Putnam's work popularizing it (1995), academic interest in civic associations and social trust has surged (Skocpol and Fiorina 1999). Many scholars share the common goal of explaining the residuals left by rational choice explanations of politics and policy (Edwards and Foley 1998). Dissatisfied with, on the one hand, unidimensional portrayals of political behavior at the individual level, and, on the other hand, the dry institutionalism of state-centered studies, researchers wish to bring civil society and culture back into the picture.

The historical-institutionalist approach advocated by Theda Skocpol lends itself to this focus on the promise and shortcomings of civic explanations of policy outputs, moving as it does beyond the social psychological or cognitive perceptions of individuals. As Skocpol and Fiorina put it, "From a historical-institutionalist perspective, the trouble with

American democracy today does not lie in sheer social disconnection, nor simply in the generalized growth of social and political distrust. Institutionalists examine changing patterns or [sic] organization and resource balances. They ask who relates to whom, and who is organized for what purposes" (1999). This chapter adopts a similar approach, showing how civic engagement and voluntarism—what I refer to as civic environmentalism—can have a decidedly local and environmental orientation. Civic environmentalism provides an important, local complement to (and in some cases, is a driver of) governmental provision of collective environmental goods like open space.

CIVIC ENVIRONMENTALISM AND ITS FUNCTION

Dewitt John views civic environmentalism as a bottom-up, grassroots approach, whereby communities and states largely influence their own policies to protect the environment without being forced to do so by the federal government (1994). In John's view, civic environmentalism evolved to address the shortcomings of federal environmental laws. In the 1970s, the top-down, command and control, "gorilla-in-the-closet" approach began with the formation of the EPA. According to John, the weak enforcement of federal laws during the 1980s encouraged civic environmentalism, starting with the cutbacks of the EPA budget during the Reagan era and continuing with the stalemate between the president and Congress. In his view, Washington gridlock prompted local and state groups to address the "unfinished business" of federal environmental policy, including pollution prevention, non-point-source pollution, and restoration and protection of ecosystems. John argues that these issues lend themselves to nonregulatory policy tools, which provide information and incentives rather than sanctions.

But John emphasizes that civic environmentalism works with traditional regulatory policies rather than replacing them. Local and state governments are better suited to providing customized regulation appropriate to their areas. They also tend to start with consensual, rather than confrontational, approaches. The federal government still plays a role in these areas, but as "a gatherer, a sifter and distributor of information" (ibid., p. 286), and a funding source. The federal government also functions as a background threat that will step forward if states fail to come through.

William Shutkin, in The Land That Could Be, focuses less on the absence of federal policy makers and more on the relationship between civic engagement, social capital, and local environmental protection:

"Civic environmentalism is based on the notion that environmental quality and economic and social health are mutually constitutive and that the protection of the environment where one lives and works is directly connected to and as important as the protection of wilderness areas or wetlands. Civic environmentalism confronts the irony that most Americans seem to care more about protecting remote natural areas than the very places they inhabit" (2000, p. 14). Drawing on both these views, we can see that what is civic about civic environmentalism is that it is used *for* collective or public goods and *by* nongovernmental organizations, local government, or more loosely organized volunteers. It is environmental in the sense that residents participate, volunteer, and network specifically on behalf of environmental goods, rather than any other social benefit. Civic environmentalism consists of a social and political resource that is usually latent, diffuse, and subtle in its uses. That is, policy makers, agency officials, and nongovernmental organizations can and do draw on the resources of civic voluntarism, environmentalism, and community spirit to legitimate their arguments for public goods. A highly engaged local citizenry is also more likely to mobilize on behalf of cherished causes, although *which* causes will vary from place to place.

As Margaret Levi (1996) points out, it is essential to develop causal mechanisms by which political-cultural factors (social capital, in her example) are produced, maintained, and expanded. By the same token, more work must be done before we can conceive of the ways in which public beliefs and policy preferences might actually help civil society produce collective or public goods. Note that the goal here is not to explain how civic factors single-handedly create collective goods; rather, first we must establish whether they do make a contribution, then see how they interact with the state and markets to produce policy outcomes.

Putnam's work on social capital in the United States focuses on the incidence of civic engagement and social trust, nationally and regionally. He also cites work suggesting that, where the incidence of social capital is relatively high, desirable public "externalities" accrue to a community—lower crime, better school performance, even improved public health (Putnam 1995). Bob Edwards and Michael W. Foley (1998) argue strongly that scholars should focus on the particular benefits conferred in specific contexts by specific forms of political-cultural resources like social capital. This argument implies that there may not be generalized forms of civic engagement that can be appropriated for any and all social goals.

We should therefore look at civic environmentalism in specific contexts, posing questions about the nature of social networks affecting well-bounded issues. I suggest the following mechanisms by which civic environmentalism might serve as a resource contributing to public benefits in the environmental issue area. Civic environmentalism creates

1. an expectation (or desire) for public or collective environmental goods and services. To the extent that they desire collective goods, people may be characterized as "other-regarding." They may become other-regarding partly as a consequence of dealing with the needs and demands of others not like themselves. Such expectations, in turn, develop

2. a means by which to provide public goods and services, or to at least facilitate the provision of goods and services at a lower cost of time, money, energy, policing, monitoring, or organizing than would be provided privately or by the state acting alone. These modes of producing public goods and services are reinforced by

3. positive experiences demonstrating the effectiveness of associations and social networks in civil society at providing collective goods and services.

The first factor includes preferences for both public benefits and environmental protection. For example, how does a community view the role of local government? Is land acquisition a legitimate, even desirable, pursuit of local government? Is taxation a desirable policy tool for achieving land preservation, or should citizens work through private organizations using private resources?

A look at voting on statewide ballot initiatives helps us assess the variation on this factor. For example, California voters passed (by 56 percent) the latest of three antitax initiatives in November of 1996 (Proposition 218). Only four counties failed to pass this initiative; not surprisingly, these include three San Francisco Bay Area counties (Alameda, Marin, and San Francisco). Residents in these counties tend to support relatively higher local taxes, demand high levels of public services, and protect relatively large tracts of local open space at public expense.

My community and conservation survey (appendix 2) operationalizes this "expectations" factor with questions gauging the importance of environmental quality to respondents' choices about where they live, and with questions measuring their expectations for local government (more or less spending for services, more or less regulation on development). Familiarity with and participation in land trust activities is particularly important, since land trusts have acquired or brokered acquisitions of at least half the total local open space protected in California. Moreover, land trusts can act more quickly than local or state agencies, especially when unexpected opportunities for land acquisition deals arise. They also help mobilize support for local and statewide ballot measures that raise funds for park and open space purchases.

I chose the second factor, a means by which to provide collective environmental goods, because it is closely related to civic engagement, so often cited as a critical social resource. The "parks capacity" index I constructed for this factor uses survey questions, aggregated to the county level, measuring (1) informational resources, such as knowledge of development or land use problems and conflicts, and familiarity with land trusts, (2) financial resources in the form of willingness to pay for collective environmental goods, either directly, in the form of property taxes, or indirectly, in the form of income tax for park bond issues, (3) participation in a wide variety of face-to-face activities, (4) nongovernmental organization resources in the form of volunteer activity for civic and environmental causes, and (5) a county's average vote on statewide environmental measures, 1924–2000 (see appendices 3 and 4 for these index components).

The third factor measures people's ratings of the effectiveness of civil society at providing collective environmental goods. Knowing that the riverbanks and beaches one visits are clean and healthy in part because of adopt-a-creek or -beach efforts reinforces the notion that volunteer activities are viable, effective ways to maintain a cherished resource. Similarly, if repeated efforts to influence a local planning commission or a city council generally result in positive outcomes, one is likely to conclude that such outreach is worthwhile. People can also experience effectiveness if they have personally had success (say, in protecting land from development) or if their faith and trust in civic leaders proves to be well-founded over time. For this measure of effectiveness, I first used questions gauging the quality and number of local parks and youth programs. I then gauged *unwillingness* to pay extra property taxes for local parks and open space. Specifically, I used replies that demonstrated a lack of faith in public spending or local government officials (see appendix 5 for an explanation of how the indices were constructed). Table 4 shows how these three components of civic environmentalism are related at the individual level, as measured by the community and conservation survey.

At the individual level, these factors are only somewhat related, but as table 5 shows, at the county mean level, the relationships are quite strong, and they take the directions expected by the model.[1]

TABLE 4. CORRELATION MATRIX
OF CIVIC FACTORS, INDIVIDUAL LEVEL

	Government effectiveness	Parks capacity	Environmental awareness
Government effectiveness	1.000		
Parks capacity	0.173	1.000	
Environmental awareness	0.136	0.438	1.000

SOURCE: "The Community and Conservation in California Survey Questionnaire" (see appendix 2).
NOTE: N = 2,977 respondents.

TABLE 5. CORRELATION MATRIX
OF CIVIC FACTORS, COUNTY MEANS

	Government effectiveness	Parks capacity	Environmental awareness
Government effectiveness	1.000		
Parks capacity	0.561	1.000	
Environmental awareness	0.516	0.766	1.000

SOURCE: "The Community and Conservation in California Survey Questionnaire" (see appendix 2).
NOTE: N = 30 counties.

LOCAL VARIATION

Most studies of political or civic culture use data aggregated at the national level; occasionally, researchers collect data at the state level (Rice and Sumberg 1997). Data on civic engagement and associational life are based on national surveys taken over the last thirty to forty years. These data are appropriate for marking the patterns of change throughout American society; however, they cannot be used to distinguish at a far smaller scale, such as between communities. Indeed, the premise of the policy capacity framework I introduced in chapter 1 is that local political cultures and institutional performance vary tremendously in the United States, suggesting that researchers may learn a great deal about participatory democracy if they change their scale, units of analysis, and resolution to a subnational, substate level.

Until the last decade or so, however, sociologists and political scientists have downplayed the relevance of local politics, perhaps overstating the homogenizing effects of national systems of education, mass media, and big government (Urry 1990). This trend is being reversed, especially in policy studies whose object of attention is services and outputs in general and policy variation in particular (Sharpe and Newton 1984). Studying local outputs permits a wealth of comparisons unavailable to national or area studies, and comparative studies of *environmental* policy outputs and protection activities are becoming more common and sophisticated (Ringquist 1993; Ringquist et al. 1995; Williams and Matheny 1995).

John A. Agnew (1987) points out that local government in the United Kingdom and the United States is sufficiently autonomous and differentiated that a focus on place, whether a political jurisdiction or a specific community, can help construct persuasive explanations of variations in local policy outputs. In another example, Sharpe and Newton observe that Welsh counties distinguished themselves from English ones by their much higher per capita spending on local government services. The authors argue that "cultural differences" might partly determine public policy, since these patterns of spending "could not be reduced entirely to such things as class, politics, grants, sparsity, or the agricultural basis of the economy" (1984, p. 172).

Using measures of civic culture and government performance, Tom W. Rice and Alexander F. Sumberg found that states with highly developed civic cultures were more likely to score highly on measures of government performance.[2] Similarly, a 1993 study of political participation, *The Rebirth of Urban Democracy* by Jeffrey M. Berry and colleagues, demonstrates that a focus on politics and associations at the neighborhood level can yield rich, comparative insights about the nature of meaningful participation and the relationship between a central policy making authority (city hall) and citizen interests. This promise is echoed by Bruce A. Williams and Albert R. Matheny: "By studying the ways in which citizens respond to policies that impose significant costs and, less frequently, benefits on their communities, the investigator can clarify many issues of participation and democracy obscured by a focus on national policy-making" (1995, p. 10).

In pursuing this research agenda on civic engagement and institutional performance, it is important to explore whether a strong civic culture raises the quality and pace of collective action across social issues or manifests itself differently across issues and communities. In the environmental arena, it is reasonable to expect that high levels of civic engagement and voluntarism will translate into sustained collective efforts to protect the environment. For example, citizens who mobilize to work on single-issue environmental problems often go on to participate in other policy arenas (Press 1994; Szasz 1994). In its 1994 survey of giving and volunteering in the United States, the Independent Sector (a nongovernmental organization dedicated to voluntarism and philanthropy) found that respondents who reported contributing to environmental causes were far more likely to be members of civic or voluntary associations, professional societies, or political organizations (Hodgkinson et al. 1995, p. 90).

CIVIC ENVIRONMENTALISM IN CALIFORNIA

As expected, civic environmentalism does vary at the local level in California. Three sets of observations support this claim. First, there are many local nongovernmental organizations dedicated to land preservation in California, but their distribution is by no means uniform. Second, voters in counties across the state vary tremendously in their support for environmental policies at the polls. Third, respondents to my community and conservation survey also vary, by county, in their environmental attitudes and expectations as well as their civic activities.

Chapter 2 provided several examples of organized civic environmentalism at work on the local level in California. This is generally replicated across the United States, where many public activities and services are now being carried out or provided as a result of partnerships between nongovernmental organizations, loosely organized citizens, and administrative agencies (Kettl and Milward 1996). From problem recognition to policy formation, budgeting, implementation, and monitoring, the line between official governance and voluntarism is becoming increasingly blurred.

In the past twenty years, local residents in California have increased the roles they play in managing their local environments. There are now approximately 600 environmental groups in California characterized as "non-profit corporation, non-governmental organization, or citizen group" (Harbinger Communications 1998). The Land Trust Alliance lists 125 separate land trusts in the state of California having primary responsibility for protecting about 570,000 acres. Adding the organizations discussed in chapter 2 permitted me to "assign" land preservation groups to specific counties when the bulk of their efforts were local.

Land preservation organizations are not evenly distributed, however, as illustrated by figure 20, which shows the frequency of nongovernmental organizations per county. Fully half of these organizations are

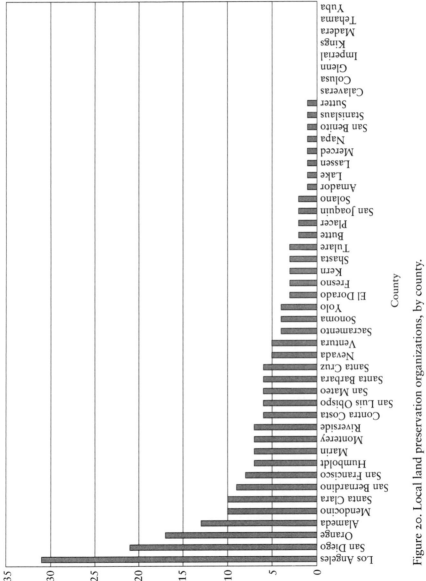

Figure 20. Local land preservation organizations, by county.

based in only eight of California's fifty-eight counties, although they do not always confine their activities to a single county.

CIVIC ENVIRONMENTALISM
AND LOCAL OPEN SPACE PRESERVATION

If civic environmentalism does vary throughout the state, to what extent does it contribute positively to local land preservation? I rely on macro- and microlevel data to answer this question.

Recall that there are many land preservation organizations throughout the state, but they are unevenly distributed geographically. Figure 21 shows that land preservation organizations are associated with increased land preservation. This result is consistent with the policy capacity formulation of chapter 1. The sheer number of land preservation organizations probably helps a county and region protect more land; it also permits specialization among different groups. Organizations like the local chapters of the League of Women Voters can bring considerable, seasoned experience in political mobilization to new issues, including land preservation.

The long sweep of the state's experiment with direct democracy has enabled voters to express their environmental policy preferences scores of times, especially in the period since 1962, and these elections permit yet another macrolevel glimpse into the relationship between civic factors and land preservation. Ballot propositions also allow scholars and political strategists a rare glimpse into realized, as opposed to stated, policy preferences. By my count, voters in California have been presented with environmental policy measures seventy times since 1924, with the vast majority of these occurring since 1960.[3] These include parkland acquisition, water or mass transit bonds, and regulatory measures concerning coastal zone management, oil drilling in state lands, gill net fishing, water quality protection, toxic materials management, bottle deposits, and wildlife habitat conservation. For all but six of these measures, the "yes" vote was the pro-environmental choice (see appendix 4 for a list of the measures). A little over two-thirds of these measures (fifty) were approved along pro-environmental lines. As mentioned in chapter 2, twenty-one of the seventy measures were park bonds or contained provisions for substantial park- and habitat land acquisition funds.

County-level returns from the seventy measures on the ballot since 1924 reveal that electoral support for the environment varies considerably around the state. While average state approval was 55 percent, sup-

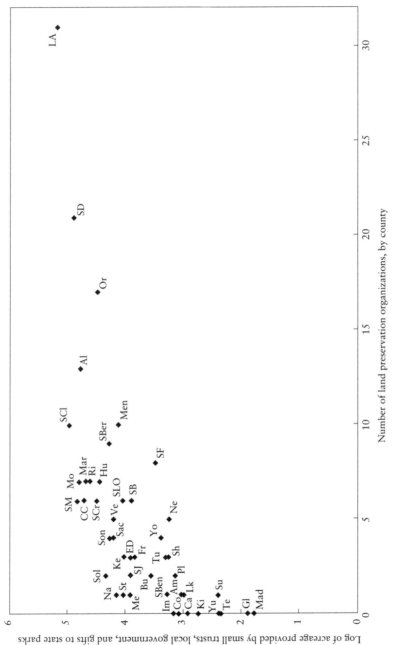

Figure 21. Relationship between nongovernmental preservation organizations and land preservation, 2000. (*N* = 47 counties, *R* = 0.66) A list of county abbreviations can be found on p. xi.

TABLE 6. CORRELATION COEFFICIENTS FOR COUNTY AVERAGE APPROVAL RATES OF STATEWIDE ENVIRONMENTAL BALLOT MEASURES, BY MEASURE TYPE

	Wildlife	Parks	Coastal protection	Clean water	Water conservation	Energy	Toxics	Transit	Gas tax	General
Wildlife	1.000									
Parks	0.909	1.000								
Coastal protection	0.875	0.944	1.000							
Clean water	0.876	0.929	0.823	1.000						
Water conservation	0.877	0.929	0.832	0.972	1.000					
Energy	0.737	0.825	0.837	0.773	0.778	1.000				
Toxics	0.836	0.834	0.828	0.761	0.786	0.699	1.000			
Transit	0.881	0.920	0.821	0.904	0.950	0.709	0.817	1.000		
Gas tax	0.826	0.915	0.875	0.903	0.926	0.786	0.868	0.934	1.000	
General	0.823	0.850	0.814	0.799	0.856	0.732	0.892	0.827	0.898	1.000

SOURCE: California Secretary of State 2000.
NOTES: N = 58 counties, P-values for all correlations are <0.0001.

port for the pro-environment position ranged from a little under 36 percent in Modoc (a far northern, rural county) to about 69 percent in the city and county of San Francisco (see figure 22). Voting returns on these propositions shows that citizens in California counties tend to vote consistently for or against environmental propositions. Thus, local patterns of environmentalism, at least those measured by these electoral returns, are persistent over time *and* vary from county to county.

Before seeing whether local, generalized support for environmental protection policies is correlated with land preservation, we need to know whether environmental issues were "bundled," that is, whether voters tended to treat different subcategories of environmental measures roughly the same. If environmental issues were indeed bundled, then a composite score, consisting of a county's average support for all statewide environmental policy measures, can be used as a robust predictor of land preservation.

Taking average county approval rates for environmental measures in ten categories, I correlated mean county approvals of measures in each category, the results of which appear in table 6. I included in these ten categories only environmental policy issues for which there had been more than one measure on the ballot since 1911. The high correlations in table 6 suggest that voters appear to treat most environmental measures as one policy type.

Strong support at the ballot for statewide environmental measures correlates quite well with local open space preservation (see figure 23). This suggests that voters support environmental protection, including land conservation, at both the state and local levels, and that environmental policy support is likely to influence a community's capacity to mount park acquisition and maintenance programs.

San Francisco—city and county—consistently supports environmental measures by the largest of state margins. Because it is a small, entirely developed county, San Francisco skews the data in figure 23. Removing San Francisco (and thereby including only counties that have substantial amounts of acreage left in an undeveloped state) results in an appreciably stronger relationship between environmental support at the polls and land preservation ($R = 0.77$).

To summarize, the electoral data demonstrate that environmental policy support varies from county to county, is bundled across environmental issue type, remains fairly consistent through time, and relates strongly to local land preservation. We now turn to another measure of civic environmentalism using survey data.

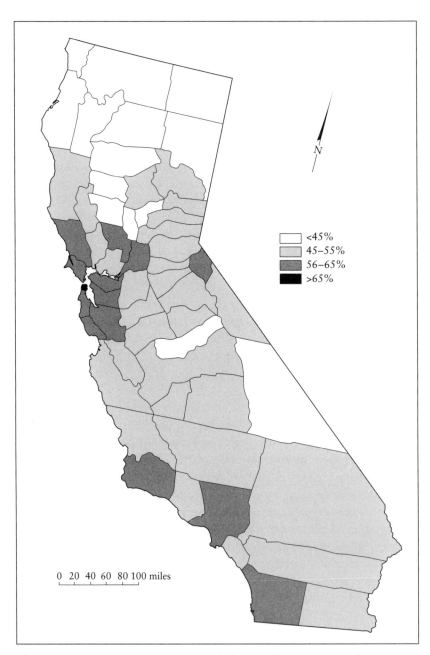

Figure 22. Average county-level approval of statewide environmental measures, 1924–2000.

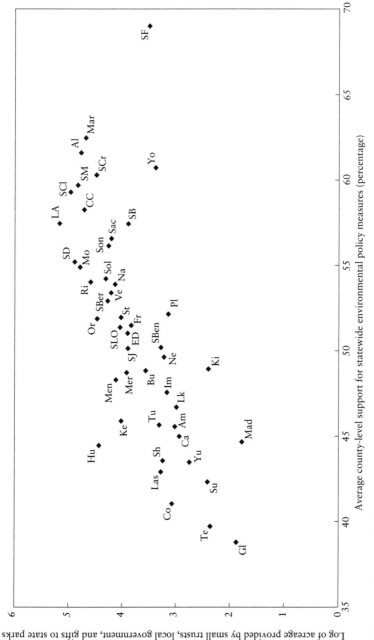

Figure 23. Relationship between voting for statewide environmental measures and land preservation, 1962–2000. ($N = 48$ counties, $R = 0.66$) A list of county abbreviations can be found on p. xi.

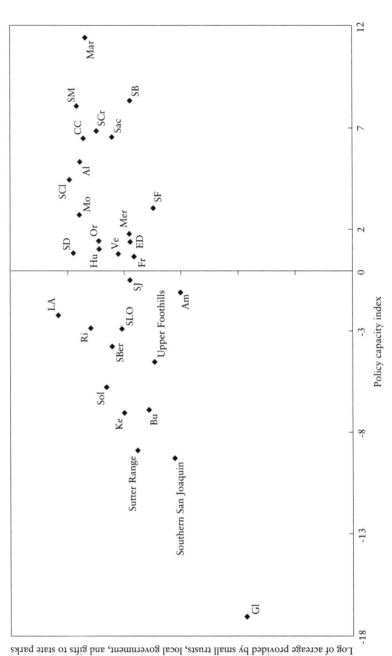

Figure 24. Relationship between policy capacity and land preservation, 2000. (*N* = 27 counties and 3 regions, *R* = 0.64) A list of county abbreviations can be found on p. xi.

Earlier we saw that high expectations of environmental goods and services can help mobilize political participation on behalf of the environment. In turn, I expect local policy capacity, which includes a community's desire for environmental goods and its ability to deliver those goods, to be strongly associated with local land preservation. Specifically, local civic environmentalism not only attracts support for political leaders advocating slow growth or preservation but also actually provides some of the technical, political, and economic resources for preservation programs.

My approach for correlating policy capacity to land preservation is first to draw on the parks capacity measure in my community and conservation survey. Recall that my measure of average parks capacity within a county consists of survey responses that indicate residents' willingness to pay more property taxes for open space, to approve state parks measures, to volunteer in civic and environmental organizations, to participate in local politics as well as in many different kinds of face-to-face activities, and to voice their opinions on the proper role of local government vis-à-vis land use regulation and growth control.

Here we will switch to a thirty-county data set, because the survey had usable samples from only thirty counties. Using mean county-level responses to the questions making up the parks capacity index, figure 24 shows the relationship between a county's open space capacity and its land preservation.

A COMPREHENSIVE MODEL

Thus far I have presented bivariate relationships to demonstrate the relationship between the land preservation problem and development pressure, fiscal and administrative resources, landscape features, and civic factors. The policy capacity concept suggests synergies between these factors; accordingly, I bring them together here. Since most of the factors I explored correlate highly with open space preservation and with each other, the many independent variables available for multivariate analyses are likely to exhibit fairly high levels of collinearity.

For example, the development measure "new housing permits, 1965-1995," is very highly correlated ($R = 0.94$ in the 47-county data set) with revenues for the same time period. This is not surprising, since new construction adds substantially to the local tax base. Similarly, the number of land preservation organizations correlates strongly with a county's administrative capacity ($R = 0.84$ in our 47-county data set), suggesting

TABLE 7. POLICY CAPACITY AND OPEN
SPACE REGRESSION MODELS

Model Variables	Model adjusted R^2	P-values
Policy capacity and landscape effects	0.765	
Policy capacity		0.001
Log urban river meters		<0.001
Log urban mean elevation		0.0364
Policy capacity, landscape effects, and administrative capacity	0.79	
Policy capacity		0.0007
Log urban river meters		0.0001
Administrative capacity		0.007
Landscape effects and administrative capacity	0.685	
Log urban river meters		<0.0001
Administrative capacity		0.0383
Policy capacity, landscape effects, and development pressure	0.75	
Policy capacity		0.0019
Log urban river meters		0.0084
Development pressure		0.0936
Policy capacity and local revenues	0.63	
Policy capacity		0.0004
Log local revenues, 1965–1996		0.0001
Administrative capacity, landscape effects, and development and revenue index	0.79	
Administrative capacity		0.0059
Log urban river meters		<0.0001
Development plus revenue index		0.0484

SOURCES: California Governor's Office of Planning and Research 1999; California Secretary of State 2000; "The Community and Conservation in California Survey Questionnaire" (see appendix 2); United States Geological Survey 2000.

NOTES: The dependent variable in all models is the log of local government and small land trust and local state park gift acres. $N = 27$ counties and 3 regions.

the two share a common social or labor pool of technical and organizational resources. Solid approval of environmental measures within a county also correlates strongly with the county parks capacity measure (R = 0.685, N = 30 counties). Not surprisingly, these strong intercorrelations skew the expected results in multiple regressions, in effect rendering many of the independent variable contributions insignificant.

I therefore propose several models in table 7. Most make use of the parks capacity index described earlier in the chapter. As the table shows, the policy capacity concept I introduced in chapter 1 is fairly robust—the various models all result in R^2 *values above 0.6, and most of them are 0.75 or above.*

The policy capacity concept suggests it is unlikely that any one factor can make or break the acquisition of open space, and the various model specifications in table 7 demonstrate the concept's robustness. As I explained earlier in this chapter, counties need not be among the wealthiest to protect even expensive parcels, provided there is a strong showing of other factors, such as particularly supportive taxpayers willing to make sacrifices. Moreover, local land preservation occurs in an institutional context often shaped by state and federal opportunities or constraints.

Given a model of social relations in which voluntarism and "good" attitudes lead to good and democratic outcomes, it is tempting to attribute too much autonomy to civil society. Politics and policy happen at the intersection of the state, market, and civil society; no one sector operates fully apart from the other or in wholly different ways (i.e., through hierarchies or voluntary exchanges). What is quite clear from the example of California is that open space preservation frequently occurs with the help of nongovernmental organizations and loosely organized volunteers. There is also wide variation in the amount of preservation that occurs throughout the state (with or without nongovernmental organizations and voluntarism) and in how much the local citizens support these efforts. In terms of the mechanism I offered, civic environmentalism plays an important role as a pool of motivation and capacity that *can* be marshaled in the service of strong policy preferences. Civic efforts rarely take place on tracks wholly parallel to and apart from local or state government.

Armed with these encouraging results, we now turn to policy entrepreneurship—not to find different or additional explanations, but to understand how the factors examined here motivate and support leadership in land preservation.

CHAPTER 5

Policy Entrepreneurship

Communities all across the country face development pressure, and an increasing number of their citizens express deep resentment at the costs of urban sprawl. For a community to protect lands before they can be swallowed up by the growth machine depends on having more than a strong tax base and a supportive community: it requires leadership. The development pressure, landscape features, local finance, and local environmentalism I discussed in the preceding chapters create the context for such leadership. This chapter shows how local civic leaders address the land preservation challenge—how they take advantage of (or are stymied by) the local environmental, social, and fiscal contexts they must use. The essential message of this chapter is that policy entrepreneurs in this issue area have in common a set of skills and resources.

Local policy entrepreneurs are an eclectic bunch. Some have made careers of leadership, running for office or directing well-heeled foundations, land trusts, and blue-ribbon commissions; others chance upon entrepreneurship as a by-product of a campaign against a particular development project or policy change. Thus, local preservation entrepreneurs come from the ranks of dedicated activists, elected officials, appointees, and businesspeople. They include anyone consistently contributing ideas, resources, time, and energy to the task of land preservation.

Mark Schneider and colleagues identify problem-definition, risk taking, and networking skills as the minimum set of resources required by policy entrepreneurs:

TABLE 8. ENTREPRENEURIAL SKILLS
AND RESOURCES

Entrepreneurial asset	Examples
Networking	Political connections; negotiation, bargaining, or brokering skills
Problem definition and political mobilization	A vision for local or regional landscapes; skills in framing issues, defining new problems, or changing opinions about problems; access to media or a bully pulpit; ability to mobilize mass or constituent support
Technical expertise	Legal, financial, natural science (ecological, hydrological), or real estate expertise and credibility
Fund-raising	Fund-raising skills in public and private sectors
Persistence	Tenacity and a long-term local presence

All entrepreneurs must perform three functions. First and foremost, entrepreneurs discover unfulfilled needs and select appropriate prescriptions for how those needs may be met—that is, they must be alert to opportunities. Second, as they seize these opportunities, entrepreneurs bear the reputational, emotional, and frequently, the financial risk involved in pursuing a course of action with uncertain consequences. Finally, entrepreneurs must assemble and coordinate teams or networks of individuals and organizations that have the talents and/or resources necessary to undertake change. (Schneider, Teske, and Mintrom 1995, p. 2)

John W. Kingdon adds that entrepreneurs must have some claim to a hearing: "This claim has one of three sources: expertise; an ability to speak for others, as in the case of a leader or powerful interest group; or an authoritative decision-making position, such as the presidency or a congressional committee chairmanship" (1995, p. 180). Michael Mintrom adds that entrepreneurs "must be able to argue persuasively," and often must be able to make different arguments to different groups (2000, p. 60). The health and transportation policy entrepreneurs that Kingdon studied were also extraordinarily persistent: "Many potentially influential people might have expertise and political skill, but sheer tenacity pays off" (1995, p. 181).

Table 8 summarizes the entrepreneurial skills and resources that the policy literature suggests we should expect to find, and which were indeed present in the land preservation cases. Most successful preservation entrepreneurs possess several of these characteristics. However, just as all the resource elements of policy capacity (especially money and civic environmentalism) rarely coexist at very high levels in a single community, not all entrepreneurial assets are found (or needed) in great abundance in the same person. I discuss each asset in turn.

NETWORKING

The networks of open space advocates that I found crisscross local jurisdictions, class differences, and the public and private sectors. Open space entrepreneurs rarely can afford to be insular: even the most strident activists have reason to work with elected officials and business owners. Equally important, policy entrepreneurs "must be able to mix in a variety of social and political settings, so that they can readily acquire valuable information and use their contacts to advantage in pursuit of policy change" (Mintrom 2000, p. 60). Policy networks can be differentiated by the sorts of people in them as well as by how entrepreneurs use their networks.

Although conservationists are not a large group, land preservation networks vary from community to community. Entrepreneurs form and use networks specific to their needs. Private land trusts tend to put businesspeople on their boards—these may include realtors, finance experts, attorneys, ranchers, and even developers. Whether from a sense of noblesse oblige or because of environmental leanings, these board members bring their financial acumen and political access to the land trust and help endow it with a nonthreatening profile. Indeed, a major goal of many land trust directors is to use their networks to portray their organizations as mainstream, sensible, and credible; in fact, a more conservative land trust may try to distance itself from environmental organizations perceived as critical of local land uses.

Some of this credibility comes from a "revolving door" between local government and nongovernmental organizations engaged in land conservation. Environmental activists sometimes get elected to city councils or boards of supervisors based on their well-known slow-growth track record. In other cases, officials have left elected office to run a land trust or state environmental agency. The newly appointed director of the Land Trust for Santa Clara County provides a case in point. She had practiced real estate law for a number of years and found working for a private land trust to be a logical extension of her previous work. "My friends in the development community understand," she stated. "I'm just another buyer on the market. So they're okay with it."

In contrast, a land use watchdog such as the Committee for Green Foothills or LandWatch Monterey County is more likely to network with local activists, elected officials, planners and other policy analysts, and the media. Gary Patton, executive director of LandWatch, described his local, activist board of directors:

> Their chairman now works over in the Silicon Valley, but he had been the general manager of Sea Studios in Cannery Row and very oriented towards ocean and marine protection, and [he] was on the Save Our Shores board of directors for many years. . . . There's a professional planner who works for the air district on the board. There's an architect on the board. There's a person from Carmel on the board who is a member of the Big Sur Land Trust board. . . . There's a longtime political activist and a dam opponent from Carmel Valley. . . . We're actually in the last third of an outreach and diversity effort to change the board in terms of getting people of different ethnic composition and different geographic composition so the board can be more representative of a countywide constituency, since it is a countywide effort.

Leadership networks vary in public agencies as well. After the state legislature formed the new Santa Clara Open Space Authority in 1994, a citizens advisory committee was empanelled to chart the agency's first five years. In this case, diversity was a premium: committee members came from all around the agency's east and south Santa Clara County jurisdiction. They represented different ethnic groups, high-tech, labor, the local chapter of the League of Women Voters, ranching families, and environmental interests. Diversity was, in part, a strategy the executive director pursued in response to the bruising and divisive battle over the Santa Clara Open Space Authority's genesis, when a local taxpayers' association challenged the advisory vote that led to the agency's creation and its property taxation powers.[1] The diverse advisory committee also set a tone of consensus building that allows the agency to define open space broadly and inclusively. By doing so, the more urban interests could ensure that protected parcels would have access and recreation components, while environmental interests would be represented in acquisitions that slowed development and protected important habitat.

Regardless of the different interests of board or advisory committee members, there are relatively few conservation entrepreneurs, even throughout the state. Thus, there are never many "degrees of separation" between the conservation leadership of one community and another.

Everyone knows the preservation-minded elected officials, the experienced planner, the parks director who has been in her post for many years, or the environmental activist with a decade or more of experience. A Monterey County parks planner who had grown up near where he worked and had fifteen years of experience summed up his stature with a reference to the local congressman: "Sam Farr is always amazed. You know, you can ask me any question. [He says,] 'God, this guy knows everything about this county!'"

Just as the interests of people in preservation networks differ widely, so do the uses of these networks. Preservation networks allow entrepreneurs to learn and disseminate information, recruit new members, broker complex deals that cross political and public-private boundaries, and manage the interplay of local, state, and federal relations.

Much of the networking over the past two decades has involved lesson-sharing across city and county boundaries. The national Land Trust Alliance facilitates this learning for private land trusts by holding workshops, conferences, and in-depth professional seminars all over the country. Real estate and tax laws are nothing if not complex, so much so that the well-intentioned volunteer can be completely unequipped to recognize conservation opportunities when these arise, much less act on them successfully.

Local leaders consult with each other frequently, especially with sister jurisdictions in a county. Slow-growth city council members in Sonoma County convened an informal working group they whimsically called PEON (Progressive Elected Officials Network). As one city council member put it, "We just have lunch and talk about what we're doing, and [try] to see what we can do to support each other informally."

Much of this lesson-learning concerns complex land use regulation, which is the province of planning commissions, city councils, and boards of supervisors. But entrepreneurs also draw on their networks to learn about, and implement, difficult land protection deals. Because desirable parcels or ranches are often expensive and in the path of development, preservationists must be nimble, opportunistic, and creative. A seasoned entrepreneur calls on finance expertise and real estate law to make a deal happen when political windows of opportunity open.

A Marin County veteran of park acquisitions underlined the importance of networks across organizations:

> Our board for many years had an unwritten policy [for] when we were
> going to acquire, or when we wanted to acquire, land: it was kind of a third-
> third-third policy. The open space district would put up a third, we would

Figure 25. The Bear Creek Redwoods, Santa Clara County. Photo by Daniel Press.

find a third from another source such as the Marin Community Foundation or a state ballot measure, and then the local community would have to come up with a third as well.

Repeated success of this cost-sharing policy requires that networks between each organization be maintained and renewed on a continual basis.

Local leaders manage a creative interplay between private donors, land trusts, local government officials, and state or federal officials to protect valuable lands. Leaders of private organizations bring flexibility to land preservation. For example, they can purchase options on a parcel within days of a decision, and then hold these options until public agencies secure the funding necessary for purchase. In one such example of flexibility, the Peninsula Open Space Trust (POST) secured a $10 million loan to purchase part of the Bear Creek Redwoods in the Santa Cruz Mountains (see figure 25). POST subsequently launched a campaign to raise the money.

The Nature Conservancy (TNC) also demonstrates how flexible preservation approaches work. In some instances, the conservancy has purchased important ranches outright, placed conservation easements on the deeds, then resold the lands to local government or the private sector. The organization thereby secures the kind of protection it wants at a fraction of the acquisition cost.

Finally, entrepreneurial networks often span local, state, and federal government levels as well as connect local nongovernmental organizations and large statewide or national private conservation organizations. Cooperation is often needed at all these levels for land deals to go through. Locals may mobilize to protect a certain ranch, the state Department of Parks and Recreation may be the logical landowner, and the federal government may provide matching funds. Entrepreneurs must line up these actors in a reasonable amount of time and hold delicate coalitions together, often in the face of competing land use goals.

In Santa Cruz County, Fred Keeley, a local supervisor, quickly rose to a position of respect and influence after being elected to the state's eighty-member assembly, where he eventually became speaker pro tem. By virtue of his work in the legislature's resources and budget committees, Assemblymember Keeley was able to help local officials and activists augment relatively modest city and county funds with state appropriations. Thus, Keeley's departure from the local political scene extended the county's environmental policy capacity instead of diminishing it.

PROBLEM DEFINITION AND POLITICAL MOBILIZATION

As problems rise to the top of political agendas, policy entrepreneurs work hard at defining them in order to make evident these problems' importance and to attach to them their preferred solutions (Kingdon 1995, pp. 142–43). Open space entrepreneurs often accomplish this by relating what Deborah Stone calls a "story of decline": "In the beginning, things were pretty good. But they got worse. In fact, right now, they are nearly intolerable. Something must be done." She goes on to say, "This story usually ends with a prediction of crisis . . . and a proposal for some steps to avoid the crisis. The proposal might even take the form of a warning: Unless such-and-such is done, disaster will follow" (1997, p. 138). In the open space case, entrepreneurs can bring to this story a compelling element of redemption offered by the landscapes themselves. So many Californians are inspired by the beauty of their state that they react positively to pictures of open vistas, forested hills, or deserts in bloom. Thus their story is a variation on Stone's: "In the beginning, the state or region was unspoiled and lovingly cared for. But then too many people carelessly overdeveloped the land. We could end up like Los

Angeles, but we don't have to. If we all contribute a little (a donation, a property tax increase, or time), we will keep (or restore) the best of what's left."

A retired county supervisor from Santa Clara stressed the mobilizing power of the decline-and-redemption story: "When you begin to enunciate what sounds reasonable, sounds good, sounds positive, and you get it on the ballot and you push it and put your money and your bodies behind it, it's successful because, for one thing, it plays on the fears of people that, if you don't do this, the land's going to be raped."

While visions of large, open landscapes certainly compel local leaders to work for preservation, the landscapes themselves also serve as mobilizing resources for entrepreneurs. The solution to sprawl can be an especially tangible one, to the extent that local supporters can see or recreate in the lands they help preserve.

The vision of a problem and its solution can be compelling even when there's uncertainty about the outcomes of a given political campaign or fund drive. Commenting on the importance of seizing land-acquisition opportunities whenever they arise, one land trust director said, "It's not like you have to have 'A' to 'Z' completed." Her assistant added, "I always know what 'Z' is. 'Z' is a beautiful property that's been restored to its natural condition . . . [and about to receive] the best possible management for the next twenty years. And 'A' is, you've got to get it [the property] first."

As the open space planning experience throughout the twentieth century suggests, entrepreneurial vision can sometimes be grand and sweeping. Instead of groping along incrementally, policy entrepreneurs in the open space arena can sometimes bring about what Nancy C. Roberts and Paula J. King (1996) call "radical change by design." For example, the greenbelt around the city of Santa Cruz, put in place by radical local leaders of the 1970s and 1980s, represented not only a significant policy innovation but also a land use program aimed in a direction opposite to that in which the city and county had been headed for the previous twenty years.

A radical design may be nothing more (or less) than a preservation plan for a watershed, foothill range, or river. Preservationists in the public and private sectors commonly adorn their offices and brochures with pictures or maps of their priority and target landscapes. A picture of a beautiful vista is thus always on hand when potential donors come calling on a land trust or park acquisition director. Taking philanthropists on tours of desirable properties achieves the same effect—it is easy to see how a person's experience as a good realtor would play a role in "selling" a piece of land to potential benefactors.

In open space preservation, having a vision is not synonymous with being politically liberal, as one Orange County planner put it when describing a conservative supervisor, "He was a pro-development guy, but very demanding with regard to the public good in two particular respects. He was absolutely relentless in demanding, and backing us up in getting, as much regional parkland as we could from developers. The other thing he had absolutely no tolerance for was obstructions to free coastal access."

When preservation activities depend on electoral or other forms of mass support, local entrepreneurs must complement their vision with traditional coalition building and mass mobilization. One of the campaign organizers of two successful Los Angeles county parks measures stressed how comprehensive her mobilization effort had to be:

> We had a countywide citizens advisory committee for both measures. It was comprised of a pretty broad range of people: senior groups, youth groups, law enforcement, business leaders, Chamber of Commerce, environmental groups—a little bit of everybody. And that was the organization for the group that really framed the measure. They had to sign off on it. They reviewed all the different components and sent the final version to the board of supervisors. . . . We worked with every single, or almost every single, city and with hundreds and hundreds of groups throughout the county. . . . In 1996 we had, I think, over 850 different organizations—civic, law enforcement, senior, youth, school organizations—endorsing the measure.

Referring to San Diego's San Dieguito River, one open space agency director echoed this theme of broad participation: "The River Valley Land Conservancy . . . [is] involved in [volunteer activity]. That's a support organization. And we have a citizens advisory committee that is composed of approximately forty organizations. So, we have [representatives] from environmental organizations, we have property-owner representatives, we have community planning group representatives, we have neighborhood association representatives, professional association representatives; and they meet generally monthly." A compelling vision, a medium for the preservation message, a coalition to carry and sustain that message—all are mobilizing skills familiar to any student of politics. In that sense, vision, problem definition, and mobilization are *generic* political resources; for these to make a difference in land preservation, they must be matched with experience and information specific to the open space policy arena.

TECHNICAL EXPERTISE

Land preservation has become a complex pursuit. Policy entrepreneurs often preserve land because they can bring to bear the required legal, financial, scientific, or administrative expertise for a project to happen. They are rarely well trained in a single one of these fields, but rather they are likely to be expert at what Kingdon calls blending the substantive and the political as needed to make projects and programs succeed (1995, p. 37). Moreover, policy entrepreneurs often have eclectic interests and are willing to evolve as their personal and public missions require. As one parks planner on the Central Coast, originally trained in resource management, put it, "What I don't have a grasp on is the technical tools of acquisition, which is a learning thing, which I've never been afraid of."

It is not in their job description, but the preservation entrepreneurs with expertise in the processes of local land use politics and policy are invaluable. Paul Steinberg refers to this resource as process expertise, which "includes knowledge of the complex formal rules and routines of government, as well as more tacit and informal knowledge concerning the conventions of political engagement" (1999, p. 278). These processes of political engagement are especially important. When faced with a preservation challenge or opportunity, where does one start? The novice activist or councilmember will rarely sense "the art of the deal": Who should be approached for ideas? Who should be approached for funds? How should questions be framed? What is the best sequencing? If legislation comes into play, a skilled entrepreneur will be able to call on his or her sophisticated understanding of parliamentary procedure, committee jurisdiction, and coalition building. If local plans or zoning changes are involved, it is critical for policy entrepreneurs to understand exactly how decisions can and do come before planning commissions, city councils, and county supervisors.

The easiest land protection deal requires input from many actors. As one Marin County parks official pointed out, in addition to coordinating the local elected leadership, community groups, and landowners, policy entrepreneurs must "coordinate efforts of the county real estate section to prepare deeds [and] appraisals." If bonds are sold to acquire property, local officials must "deal with bond underwriters [and] . . . bond counsel, the people that actually prepare all the documents that have to be approved by the board to create these special districts. All sorts of financial advisors we have to deal with—the fiscal agents." In addition, local preservationists increasingly maintain sophisticated public information capacities, drawing on many of the same communications and political skills as the savviest public relations firms.

Even in the best of economic times and with a politically supportive electorate, local public financing is difficult and rule bound. Local government can borrow money in many different ways, through certificates of participation or lease, general or limited tax-obligation bonds, revenue anticipation notes, revenue bonds, or other creative means open to fiscally imaginative staff. These often differ in the nature of repayment, depending on the local government's fiscal rating and the source of funds. A well-informed entrepreneur can select finance mechanisms that allow for matching funds or that permit local government to seize a land-acquisition opportunity that may be inconveniently timed vis-à-vis its budget cycle. Similarly, successful open space entrepreneurs also become reasonably expert in public and private real estate law or surround themselves with real estate specialists from the planning, legal, or accounting disciplines.

By the late 1990s, most preservation organizations and parks agencies had on occasion used some kind of geographic information system. Entrepreneurs must understand enough about GIS capabilities and limitations to know whether their land trust or parks agency should have GIS expertise in-house and, if not, where to go for important mapping—and, most important, *why* to use maps. Mapping expertise is expensive, time-consuming, and complex. Good open space entrepreneurs use GIS maps to inspire donors, plan for easement monitoring, create baseline biological assessments, and prioritize new acquisition or easement activities.

Ensuring that land is well managed has become increasingly important to protection efforts, and it includes proper monitoring of conservation easements, fire control or use, grazing, fencing, removal of exotic species, and management for recreation (see figure 26). A good entrepreneur in the open space policy arena knows not only how to get land protected but also how to keep it that way. Doing so requires at least a working knowledge of the resource management appropriate to the mission of the organization or agency, as well as knowledge of what the land can support. It requires more of the process expertise introduced earlier—entrepreneurs must draw on political, legal, and social skills to make sure that lands are managed properly from the start. Increasingly, crafting appropriate land management solutions—beginning with the inception of a preservation deal and continuing with resource use—also requires knowledge of the mechanics and economics of resource extraction, management, and use. As Brian D. Richter and Kent H. Redford

Figure 26. A prescribed burn in Pogonip City Park, Santa Cruz. Photo by Victor Schiffrin.

(1999) point out, good preservation deals often entail convincing the landowners that the land's new overseers will be able to appropriately manage resources, in exchange for their cooperation in, say, setting up conservation easements.

The older land trusts and parks agencies have now found themselves with substantial acreages to manage, and so their programmatic focus is shifting. As the director of the Big Sur Land Trust in Monterey County put it, "As a land trust matures, you become more of a manager and less of an acquirer." His point was echoed by a veteran park planner in Marin County: "When we were managing a few thousand acres, [we could] get away with a lot of stuff. . . . You knew the land intimately, you knew the areas that you were in charge of."

Large holdings attract a lot of attention, as the Marin planner explained, "People want to ensure that the lands are being well taken care of. . . . We probably have throughout the county . . . about 1,700 neighbors[;] . . . each one of them has an interest, and each one of them is concerned about how the land adjacent to their property is managed, particularly with respect to fire and things that can impact their property directly."

FUND-RAISING

Fund-raising in the post–Proposition 13 era is more critical than ever. Even in the relatively good economic times of the 1990s, local preservationists had to compete with numerous organizations and governments for scarce resources. Entrepreneurs draw on a handful of fund-raising mechanisms and processes that include grant-writing, securing public funds through the budget process in local or state politics, mounting extensive campaigns for voter approval of bonds or tax and fee assessments, cultivating charitable gifts from wealthy or landowning individuals, and using other resources to leverage funds from any of the above. Some entrepreneurs focus their energies more on writing grant proposals to foundations or state or federal agencies, while others engage in private networking among the wealthy. Successful fund-raisers in the public sector also rely on more traditional political channels such as persuading a local legislator to secure money from the state budget or putting together campaigns for bond, tax, or fee measures.

The executive director of the Peninsula Open Space Trust (POST), one of the most successful regional land trusts in the country, made clear the importance of having real estate developers, contractors, land use and estate attorneys, and wealthy locals on her board. Normally, environmentalists view such people as the operators of the growth machine—in a word, the enemy. But these people were critical to POST's mission; without them, access to large donors would be far more difficult. That said, POST's director emphasized that fund-raising is not a job only—or primarily—for a board of trustees: "To say that it's the job of the board is wrong. It's everybody's job. . . . It's the job of the top person more than anyone else's."

Land trusts and parks agencies put much of their human resources into fund-raising because it is so uncertain. The Big Sur Land Trust director remarked, "You've got twenty different projects pending, you'll probably need three times that number [of] applications for grants going out, because no single funding source today will fund 100 percent of any project. Everybody wants someone else to participate. Packard [Foundation] wants to leverage, state [Department of Parks and Recreation] wants to leverage, everybody. So we've got to send out a lot for every project. Every project has three to five contributors and that means three to five applications have to be successful."

Marin County's park officials have joined with residents of the county's smaller cities to tailor public financing to very local needs and desires. There, residents have approved benefit assessment and community-facilities districts for open space, regularly overcoming the two-thirds majority approval requirement put in place by state law. A veteran of many open space acquisitions in that county told how reluctant voters were to pass countywide measures and stressed the importance of mobilizing electoral support for open space at local levels—sometimes smaller than cities or parks districts: "I worked with people who lived in the area to define the district, the area that would benefit by this acquisition, and then the neighbors [took] it over, [took] over the political process of informing their neighbors of this effort and getting them to sign a petition to support a special assessment within that particular area, to help pay for the open space and the improvements."

As tenuous as fund-raising for land acquisition can be, raising money for land management is often far more difficult. Some land trusts solve this problem by setting up management endowments when they purchase lands or conservation easements. Others, like the Marin County Open Space District, find themselves dedicating most of their operating budget to land management in some years, leaving very little for new land purchases: "That forces us to look outside, to use OPM—other people's money—which we've been really good at. I do a ratio every year with the acquisitions summary that I prepare for our board, . . . and it's always a very good ratio. I mean, some years it's $3 of other people's money to $1 of the district['s], and some years it's $7 of other people's money to $1 of the district['s]."

Land management fund-raising will certainly distinguish public and private preservation organizations in the future. Some trusts and agencies will forgo land acquisitions—even outright gifts of land—if they are not accompanied by endowments for management and liability insurance. That kind of response irks other preservationists, who argue that a gift of land should never be refused. Refusing a gift demonstrates "the vision of a pea," scoffed one San Francisco Bay Area trust director; she preferred a bolder, more opportunistic (and riskier) approach, certain that her energetic board and staff would eventually find the necessary funds for any worthwhile acquisition.

PERSISTENCE

The final characteristic and resource of the policy entrepreneur is persistence. Simply put, successful policy entrepreneurs have a long-term presence both in their issue area and where they live. A long-term presence confers legitimacy and expertise on policy entrepreneurs in many distinct but related ways. First, entrepreneurs in it for the long haul are better connected to their community and, possibly, to important donors and political actors outside their community or region. Sometimes such contacts extend to family networks, especially among owners of large ranches throughout the state's exurban zones.

Second, the seasoned entrepreneur develops a reputation—good or bad, flaky or dependable—that makes her a "known quantity." An organization (and its people) who have a long-term presence develop good reputations as effective deal brokers and land managers. Such organizations or agencies often induce property owners to step forward with a land donation or preservation opportunity.

Third, the long-term entrepreneur often can afford to be patient. As a former Santa Clara County supervisor active on open space issues explained, "People who really, truly believe in something, they work at it long enough and they've got a plan for it—they're apt to make it happen." A Monterey County parks planner pointed out that it can routinely take his agency eight years to complete land preservation deals, from the time of contact to actual public access. Sometimes it can take longer: "It's almost ten years now since we embarked upon this Monterey Bay State Seashore idea and tried to create an open beachhead from the city of Monterey all the way up to the Salinas River." When asked why a particular large national land conservation organization is not as successful or aggressive in Southern California as in Northern California, one land trust director said, "Because they're headquartered in Northern California. . . . [They] send a lot of their people from the San Francisco office down there to do the work; and I can tell you, if you're doing our kind of work, and you're not from there, . . . you can do one kind of project at a time and that's it." Preservationists coming in from outside of a county to complete one big project at a time will not be around to notice the small, seemingly unrelated properties that might someday be stitched together to form one continuous piece.

A fourth benefit of persistence—related to patience—is long memory. In a rapidly changing landscape, city councils and the developments they approve come and go. And sometimes a promise to keep a parcel as open space, made as a condition of approval of a development, drops from sight. For example, when IBM wanted to expand its Almaden Valley facility on Harry Road, the former San Jose City Council member and preservationist Jerry Estruth cried foul and reminded the city that the high-tech giant had promised to keep that parcel undeveloped (*San Jose*

Mercury News 1999). A long memory also helps deal makers compile inventories of lands eligible for acquisition or some other form of protection. Institutional memory often serves to remind entrepreneurs about past successes and warn them about failures, and to indicate the patterns these may have followed.

Fifth, a sophisticated understanding of the geography and social-political landscape of a place can be obtained only over several years. Such mental maps take a lot of time to develop but are indispensable to knowing who's who in a place, "how things get done around here" (process expertise), or simply what the names of the hills, valleys, and ranches are. Successful entrepreneurs eventually become known as people who "know everything about this county."

Finally, a long-term presence ultimately makes a native (or nearly so) out of an outsider, someone who has shared experiences and history in a place. There are still veterans of open space battles in Santa Cruz County who trace their shared initiation into local politics back to the early 1970s, when the city was set to approve a large convention center and hotel complex on what is now Lighthouse Field State Park. The same can be said about Marin County and its preservation groups, as one open space district official demonstrated:

> It is the same people that tend to get involved over and over again. We've got people serving our commission now that were the instigators of the initiative to start the open space district, and certainly a half a dozen or a dozen more have left the commission or are still around . . . or are still around and still active—if not directly, then indirectly.

ENTREPRENEURSHIP AND POLICY CAPACITY ON THE SLOPES OF WOLFBACK RIDGE

How do policy entrepreneurs integrate their skills and resources with community policy capacity? The Keig property acquisition in southern Marin County illustrates how entrepreneurs respond to development pressure and local preservation support to stitch together a successful deal with multiple players.

The 94-acre ridgeline property is a developer's and environmentalist's dream landscape. Abutting the huge Golden Gate National Recreation Area—in view of Mount Tamalpais, and a few minutes from San Francisco—the property had been zoned for development in the Marin County general plan for years. Hikers and naturalists enjoyed the property, and the Marin County Open Space District (MCOSD) nervously eyed the occasional proposal for development projects. In 1994, the MCOSD looked into purchasing the property on its own but was deterred by the $1 million price tag. The district determined that it would attempt to protect parts of the property by requesting a land dedication if a developer was ever serious about a new project, and it turned its attention to other acquisitions.

The day soon came when a developer, called the Southern Marin Cohousing Group, bought an option on the land. The group's project turned out to be more expensive than its members had anticipated; moreover, local opposition to having any development on the site quickly formed. By late summer of 1998, the cohousing group was looking for a way out of their project without losing a lot of the money it had already invested, and it approached the open space district. Unfortunately, the property became more expensive with each new appraisal, and the cohousing group was actively pursuing other developers to take over their option.

Given the cost and the property's location adjacent to a national park, MCOSD concluded that the National Park Service should purchase the property and add it to the Golden Gate National Recreation Area. The cohousing group balked, anticipating that Congress would move very slowly, if ever, to acquire the property, so the district began looking for ways to hold it long enough to persuade Congress to pick up the tab.

Enter Annette Rose, an MCOSD board member and county supervisor whose district included the Keig property. Rose could see that she had all of the elements for successful preservation arrayed before her; she just had to pull them together. As Ron Miska, a veteran open space district planner, put it, the district needed

> to show significant amounts of public support for this project that we could then take to Congress and to our other funding sources. And that's when Supervisor Rose's office really helped, with their very close contacts with the community, and started making calls and informing people about this effort to try and protect this property. We got petition letters from nearby towns, community leaders, local environmental organizations; that's when the community really got involved. It started about midway through the project, when we had to show that there was significant public support. (2000)

State and federal officials expressed strong interest in the acquisition, particularly when Rose and her allies pointed out the most unusual—and fortuitous—aspect of the property's location: not only was it adjacent to a national park, but it was also a stone's throw from Marin City, a minority community that was also the poorest in Marin County.[2] As Supervisor Rose wrote in her testimony to Congress, "Nowhere else in the entire country besides Marin City could it be said that federally subsidized public housing adjoins a National Park."[3]

While Rose made the political case for acquisition, Miska began trying to solve the technical problem of holding the property long enough to raise public and private funds. The property's price tag far exceeded the district's fiscal capabilities, so the district began seeking out financial partners. One obvious prospect was the Trust for Public Land (TPL), a national organization that had raised significant funds for preservation since 1972. The MCOSD also began laying the groundwork for a possible grant application to the California Coastal Conservancy's Bay Area Conservancy Program. However, both of these organizations were hesitant to lend financial support to the effort without assurances that Congress would eventually act on the property.

Miska and others at the MCOSD felt that the plan was dead in the water. However, they soon got a break when TPL, at the open space district's continued urging, reversed course and decided to support the project. According to Miska, "Things fell into place from there. TPL took over the negotiations with the option holders, and put their Washington lobby and publicity machine into gear to obtain congressional support for the project" (Miska 2000). The fiscal puzzle started coming together as the Marin Community Foundation awarded a $500,000 challenge grant. Just a few weeks later, the MCOSD announced an $850,000 commitment and, days after that, TPL agreed to a $1 million "bridge loan." Escrow could now close on the property while Congress considered expanding the Golden Gate National Recreation Area and authorizing the funding to do so. Congress acted in October of 2000, thereby repaying TPL and the open space district.

In policy capacity terms, development pressure on a beloved landscape galvanized local residents and entrepreneurs to take advantage of a wide array of resources. Indeed, Rose and Miska would probably not have succeeded without an impressively broad coalition that included active residents, Marin County cities, community organizations, the Trust for Public Land, state and federal elected officials and agencies, a local foundation (the Marin Community Foundation), and finally, Congress itself. Miska and Rose focused and leveraged the county's political resources by using all of the entrepreneur's assets: networking and mobilization to create a broad, resilient coalition; technical expertise to find and articulate solutions for complex deals; fund-raising skills; and persistence in seeing negotiations through the inevitable rough spots.

• • •

As Mary Bryna Sanger says about policy entrepreneurs, "Exceptional people, well schooled in the substance and politics of policymaking, with the right collective identities (personality, values, motivation, knowledge, and skills) can bring about radical change at a propitious moment. Even unexceptional people can learn how to do it" (1999, p. 179).

Land preservation entrepreneurs—whether exceptional or not— come from supportive communities blessed with some of the many enchanting landscapes the state has to offer. Even though their specific talents vary widely, most leaders draw on skills familiar to entrepreneurs in the private and public sectors. Not all communities have produced and supported strong, persistent preservation leaders, but the problem of sprawl is ubiquitous throughout California. This leaves some of the cities and counties that are most vulnerable to runaway growth in the next twenty years poorly equipped to respond with major preservation efforts. The prospects for meeting future preservation needs in California's changing social and political landscape are the subject of the next, concluding, chapter.

CHAPTER 6

Policy Capacity across the Landscape

While some communities seem to be holding the line against the growth machine, others are literally losing ground. The relative newcomers in the land preservation game will be trying to catch up with runaway sprawl for some time to come. In this concluding chapter, I assess the prospects for reforming land use policies and disseminating the lessons learned by the more preservationist counties to the ones now facing development pressure and lacking extensive policy capacity.

CHARACTERISTICS OF PRESERVATIONIST COUNTIES

The data in chapters 3 to 5 strongly support the policy capacity model: counties with greater capacity were more likely to respond to the land preservation challenge than their neighbors with less capacity. Exogenous factors are important—it matters a great deal what sorts of landscapes and rivers typify a community facing rapid change, and state or federal leadership for land use reforms can make a lasting difference. Popular attitudes and behaviors endemic to a given community also matter, especially when these support—and in some cases, *create*—energetic local leaders willing to buck the growth machine. The capacity model I introduced in chapter 1 is also robust. There is no one formula for success. The mix of factors that constitute effective local capacity—that is, recognition of a problem, landscapes that inspire communities to protect them, revenue, civic environmentalism, and policy entrepreneurship—

differs, even among the counties that succeed at preserving significant amounts of acreage.

"Local" California seems, paradoxically, to be at once infinite in its variety and astonishingly similar. To the viewer crossing any one of the passes from the western Sierra to the east side, there is no question that the landscapes are different. The same is true of the state's coastal hills and valleys—the windswept Salinas Valley seems nothing like the rolling hills of Sonoma, with its oaks and vineyards. For all of California's landscape differences, however, the human imprint appears similar north to south: the strip malls and condos are virtually indistinguishable even though hundreds of miles apart.

Land preservation in the state also exhibits this paradox of variety and similarity. Viewed simply as acreages, Sonoma and Santa Cruz Counties appear to be very similar, as do Fresno and San Luis Obispo Counties. Moreover, a hiker in Rancho San Antonio regional park will encounter vistas, oaks, chaparral, and poison oak like those one will find when strolling in Foothills City Park a mile or so away. Both are in Santa Clara County, but Rancho San Antonio is owned and managed by the Midpeninsula Regional Open Space District, while Foothills City Park is owned by the city of Palo Alto and is closed to nonresidents. Further south, but still in the same western Santa Clara foothills, the Bear Creek Redwoods Open Space is held in large part by the Peninsula Open Space Trust, and no public access is yet permitted. More important than who owns these three properties, the organizations that protect them drew on different aspects of the region's policy capacity to secure their deals.

My tables and figures reveal only part of the open space story. The numbers themselves do not show that Sonoma County has invested heavily in conservation easements rather than direct acquisition, or that the opposite is true in Santa Clara County, or that the relatively numerous nongovernmental land preservation organizations operating in and near Los Angeles have not been able to set aside much land on their own. A county parks acquisitions director revealed just how different Marin County's approach is from that of Sonoma, its neighbor to the north: "If we're going to pay money, our preference is to own the land so that people can go on it and enjoy it, and so we can manage it in the way we feel most appropriate to preserve its resources."

Among those counties that have protected substantial acreages, two important differences will affect future policy capacity and preservation

TABLE 9. A TYPOLOGY OF LOCAL OPEN SPACE
PRESERVATION EFFORTS

	Entrepreneurial		
	Private	Public	Grassroots
Publicly provided open space	Type I	Type II	Type III
Privately provided open space	Type IV	Type V	Type VI

efforts. First, communities differ in emphasizing public versus private open space preservation. Santa Cruz County, for example, with its abundance of scenic redwoods but no national forest or parks, has extensive state park acreages, many of which were purchased with funds from three private organizations, the Trust for Public Land, the Packard Foundation, and the Sempervirens Fund. Only a tiny fraction of the county's protected open space was purchased with strictly local funds.

Second, communities differ in the degree to which elite entrepreneurs versus grassroots groups lead preservation efforts. Where preservation is driven more by the elite, the public may be relatively absent from land acquisition campaigns and funding. Public entrepreneurs come from city, regional, and state government, often brokering deals and drawing on their prestige as elected officials to smooth over differences or complications. Private entrepreneurs consist of the many land trust leaders around the state, as well as wealthy, well-connected businesspersons and the occasional developer.

Grassroots efforts tend to be broad based, often involve several environmental or civic organizations, and frequently campaign for public acquisition of parcels threatened by development. Leaders surely emerge from grassroots efforts, but the extent of public involvement—and the media visibility of land preservation campaigns—is greater. Grassroots efforts also predominantly exercise *negative authority*—by blocking development projects—as opposed to launching new land acquisition projects from scratch. Indeed, a typical grassroots effort begins with hasty mobilization to oppose a specific development project and to found an ad hoc group to coordinate local lobbying and protests ("Save Gray Whale Ranch," "Keep Wilder [Ranch] wild"). The grassroots protests buy private or public entrepreneurs time to work behind the scenes, where they sometimes succeed in raising funds for development or in pressuring local government to require changes in development plans.

Table 9 categorizes these efforts into six different types, types I, II, III, and IV being the most common. Public entrepreneurialism on behalf of private efforts (type V) is relatively rare, while the opposite, work undertaken outside of government (say, by land trusts) to acquire land on behalf of local government or state parks (type I), is quite common. Different policy tools are likely to work better in different communities. A type II or III community, where support for public spending may be highest, may be more willing to support local tax and bond measures. The survey results depicted in figure 27 support these differences.

Figure 27 shows how differently respondents viewed increases in government spending to provide more services versus greater regulation of private development in order to protect more open space.[1] The bars represent the percentage by which respondents in the selected counties supported greater regulation of development *over* more spending on open space. Note that respondents in places like San Francisco, Alameda, and Sacramento supported the two approaches approximately equally, whereas residents in most of the Southern California counties—with the notable exceptions of San Bernardino and Los Angeles Counties—did not do the same. My interviews supported this conclusion. For example, Orange County planners looked wistfully at the Los Angeles experience of raising funds at the ballot in 1996 and concluded, "That would never work here."

In consequence of the differences depicted in table 9, communities vary in both the number of their land preservation organizations and the number of activities these organizations undertake. A county with long-standing, "mature" institutions may very well have (1) one or more permanently funded public agencies that acquire and manage open space for multiple purposes, (2) one or more land trusts established to raise money and awareness on behalf of public parks districts or departments, and that can act more quickly to broker deals, and (3) a watchdog organization designed to lobby local government on behalf of environmentally sensitive land uses.

These coexist more or less successfully, often falling into a division of labor that plays to each organization's strengths. Relatively clear roles help agencies and organizations to complement each other when they can and to stay out of each other's way. The director of a land trust on the North Coast stated flatly, "It's our policy not to take public stands for and against development projects." While he steers his organization away from development controversies, this policy entrepreneur is very often "first on the scene" of a preservation opportunity.

Depending on the nature of environmental problems and local policy

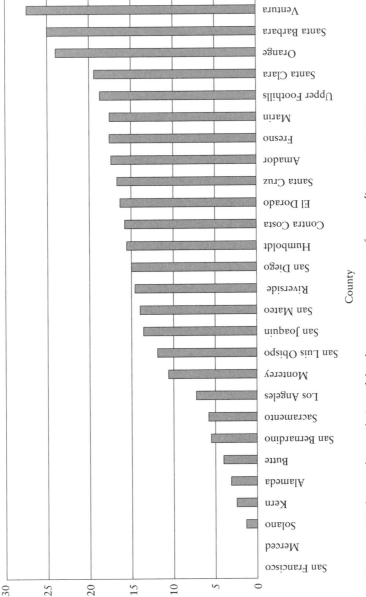

Figure 27. Preference for regulation of development over support for spending on open space.

TABLE 10. LOCAL LAND PRESERVATION ORGANIZATIONS IN SELECTED COUNTIES

	Public agencies	Private land trusts	Watchdog groups
Santa Clara	Midpeninsula Regional Open Space District, Santa Clara County Parks Department, eleven city parks departments	Peninsula Open Space Trust, Land Trust of Santa Clara County	Committee for Green Foothills, Greenbelt Alliance
Marin	Marin County Open Space District, Marin Community Service District, Marin County Department of Parks, seven city parks departments	Marin Agricultural Land Trust	Greenbelt Alliance, Bay Area Open Space Council
Alameda	Alameda Recreation and Park Department, East Bay Regional Open Space District, eleven city parks departments	South Livermore Agricultural Land Trust	Greenbelt Alliance, Bay Area Open Space Council
San Diego	San Diego County Parks Department, San Dieguito River Park Joint Powers Authority, fifteen city parks departments	Anza-Borrego Foundation, San Dieguito River Valley Land Conservancy	Save Our Forest and Ranchlands
Ventura	Conejo Recreation and Park District, Pleasant Valley Recreation and Park District, Rancho Simi Recreation and Park District, five city parks departments	Ventura County Agricultural Land Trust	Citizens to Preserve the Ojai, Save Our Agricultural Resources

capacity, some communities rely more on watchdog organizations than on land-acquiring agencies, others more on private land trusts than on regional park districts. In addition, a county with relatively weak local organizations may wish to bring in the state, as Fresno County did in the case of the San Joaquin River Conservancy. However, the idea of a state conservancy was anathema to one open space manager in San Diego County:

> I know a lot of people who are working on the San Joaquin, and they chose a state conservancy kind of mechanism, like Santa Monica and Tahoe. I guess one of the reasons that we decided we didn't want to go to the state level is because we like local control, and we think we know best what is best for us. And we want to make the bureaucracy as small as possible, . . . and we don't want to get involved in state politics. So we chose not to go that way. . . . It works, and particularly if you're going through two different counties.

Table 10 demonstrates this division of labor in five counties with numerous land preservation institutions.

EMERGING ISSUES AND TRENDS ACROSS THE UNITED STATES

Policy capacity will become increasingly important to the task of local environmental protection as any state changes and grows, but the policy context for land preservation changes constantly. Four emerging issues and trends will be especially important throughout the country in the early twenty-first century: (1) managing continued, extraordinary development pressure, (2) providing equitable access to open space, (3) managing open space in light of often competing needs and uses, and (4) cultivating local institutional capacity for effective environmental policy making and implementation.

Meeting the Growth Challenge

Unless the state and local governments adopt widespread policy changes, growth will continue at a brisk pace for years to come. Some communities have long histories of deliberately slowing growth, others have only recently (and sometimes quite reluctantly) considered reducing their development rates. In the late 1990s, many cities and counties were putting slow-growth measures on their local ballots; in California, this occurred mainly in urban, coastal counties. A few such measures appeared on ballots in the San Joaquin and Sacramento Valleys, the urbanizing Sierra

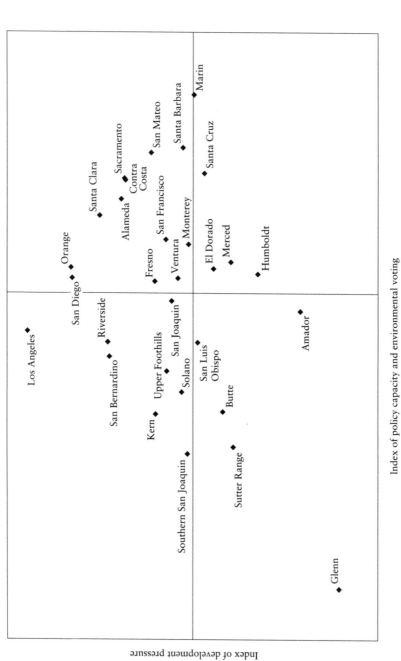

Index of policy capacity and environmental voting

Figure 28. Policy capacity and environmental voting in relation to development pressure, 2000. ($N = 27$ counties and 3 regions)

foothills, and the eastern Los Angeles basin—precisely where development pressure was at its greatest—but, with the important exception of
one in Ventura County, all failed. In contrast, most slow-growth measures
in northern California passed in the 1990s. These patterns are likely to
continue: Central Valley and Southern California respondents to the survey conducted by the Public Policy Institute of California in June 2000
were substantially less supportive of local initiatives to restrict growth
than respondents living in the San Francisco Bay Area.[2]

The rapidly developing counties in the country—around Denver,
Atlanta, Dallas, Las Vegas, and Los Angeles—entered the twenty-first
century with relatively little open space, do not enjoy landscapes as compelling as those on the coast, and face development pressure at a time
when local public financing has never been more difficult to get.[3] Figure 28 uses my survey and development data to show that many counties
with relatively less environmental policy capacity are facing strong development pressure (these are the counties situated in or near the top left
quadrant). Although the survey provided data for only twenty-seven
counties and three regions, it is clear from figure 28 that the Los Angeles
basin and the Central Valley appear to have less policy capacity to marshal in the face of development than the Central Coast and Sacramento
Valley communities.

Figure 29 tells a different, but equally important, story. In this case, I
examine the need for open space preservation from a different perspective, that of habitat protection for species at risk. In figure 29, the incidence of rare or endangered species of all taxa is on the x-axis and the
percentage of a county having some sort of protected status or public
ownership (including all public lands—local, state, federal—and all land
held by land trusts and the Nature Conservancy) is on the y-axis. If our
concern is with important habitats for the rarest species, different counties emerge as the ones to target for stepped-up protection efforts (counties in the lower right quadrant have a lot of such species and relatively
less land with some sort of protected status). Whereas figure 28 suggests
that policy capacity in some of the Central Valley and Los Angeles basin
counties must increase if these counties are to resist development pressure, figure 29 suggests that more land in the species-rich Central and
North Coast must be set aside for habitat protection to prevent extinc-
tion of many species. Similar figures could be used to identify counties
with other high-priority concerns, such as important water resources,
anadromous fish habitat, and access to open space.

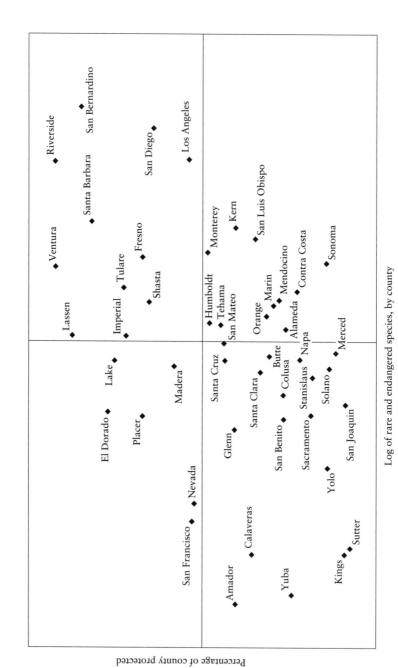

Percentage of county protected

Log of rare and endangered species, by county

Figure 29. Rare or endangered species by county versus percentage of county with protected status. ($N = 47$ counties)

Equitable Access to Open Space

Another emerging issue concerns the distribution of open space around the state. It has long been a problem that the urban poor have little access to major state and federal parks, especially those in the high Sierra. This is also a problem nearer to home, where much of the larger, prime open space abuts expensive, hillside communities and is difficult to reach from the older suburbs and downtown cores. To illustrate the disparity in open space access, I borrow a technique from environmental justice analysts. Using census and open space data, figure 30 shows the distribution of Latino residents and open space in Santa Clara County as of 1997. Note that the vast majority of the open space is concentrated in the hilly, wooded west side of the valley—where lie many of the wealthiest and whitest communities—while the east side of San Jose is home to the county's greatest number of low-income Latinos, who are far from any parks and other open spaces larger than playing fields.

Moreover, minority and poorer residents are not less interested in parks and open space than the rest of the population. If anything, Latinos were more supportive of Proposition 12, the major statewide park bond that passed in March 2000, than their white neighbors.[4] These findings are echoed in my own survey. I asked respondents to rate the number of parks in the places where they live as excellent, good, fair, or poor. Overall, about 28 percent of my respondents rated the number of parks as fair or poor, but over 36 percent of Latinos gave the number of parks in their community a fair or poor rating.[5]

Latinos also highly value open space, not just urban playing fields. My survey asked respondents, "How important are parks that maintain open space and have hiking trails, nature preserves, or campgrounds?" Of all my respondents, 63 percent rated this kind of open space as "very important"; 57 percent of the Latino respondents rated it as "very important."[6] As inner cities become further separated from exurban open space, the challenge to provide inexpensive access to the larger parks and campgrounds will become greater. It will become correspondingly more difficult to sell the idea of expensive exurban open space, purchased with public funds, to an electorate that is geographically distant from the lands.

Managing Open Space

In the rush to acquire land, good stewardship can be brushed aside. As I noted in chapter 5, proper management and its costs are increasingly

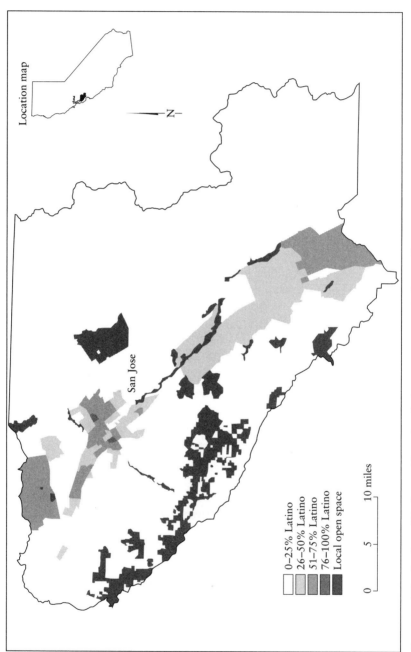

Location map

N

San Jose

0–25% Latino
26–50% Latino
51–75% Latino
76–100% Latino
Local open space

0   5   10 miles

Figure 30. Distribution of Latino residents in relation to open space in Santa Clara County, 1997.

vexing issues that local land managers must address. The first of these challenges is that of properly monitoring the many thousands of acres under conservation easements.

As the director of the Big Sur Land Trust explained, "Stewardship includes monitoring, and it's always a problem, because there's never enough time or money to monitor adequately. We have a highly processed program where we go out to see every property at least once a year—a lot of times more often." Most land trusts are not so diligent, although many are drawing on the pool of volunteers experienced with adopt-a-creek and adopt-a-park programs to create a corps of easement monitors.

As easements "age," the lands they conserve will change ownership. An attorney working for a land trust explained that owners who take title to lands with conservation easements may not have the same land ethic as the original owners:

> We try to keep track of change in land ownership, because it's not the first owner [who is a problem], it's not the one who gives the conservation easement—it's the next guy. Subsequent owners are always a problem, and in fact, my attorney associate and I gave a program at the Land Trust Alliance on enforcement because we had a couple of problems where people just thumbed their noses at it.

Much of the management problem could be alleviated by securing management funds when lands are acquired. The Big Sur Land Trust ties management funds to its acquisition program: "We have set up a stewardship endowment of a couple of million dollars to cover the cost of stewardship, and everyone that gives a conservation easement contributes a little bit to that."

Land managers today increasingly contend with conflicts over competing uses and edge effects. The first is the inevitable result of population growth and increases in the kinds of outdoor activities residents expect of their local parks and open spaces. Bitter rivalries between mountain bikers, hikers, and equestrians are legion and notorious. The second is a function not only of having more properties preserved but also of development coming to the borders of open space lands (properties abutting open space are highly prized; see figure 31).

Cultivating Policy Capacity

Preservationists across the state understand the need to cultivate policy capacity, especially in a political and fiscal climate that requires sophisti-

Figure 31. A classic greenbelt park, the Bombay property in Santa Cruz is bounded to the west by highway and ocean and to the north by farms. Photo by Victor Schiffrin.

cated policy innovations and collaborations. The three largest private players on the land preservation scene, the Trust for Public Land (TPL), the Nature Conservancy's California office (TNC), and the Packard Foundation have each implemented formal or informal mechanisms enhancing local policy capacity and augmenting their own efforts with those of local actors. The Packard Foundation Conservation Program even developed "policy, planning and capacity-building" grants aimed at increasing the staffing, planning, mobilizing, and fund-raising capabilities of small, local conservation organizations. And in the first three years of its five-year Conserving California Landscapes Initiative, the foundation spent over $168 million, mostly in grants for land acquisition (David and Lucile Packard Foundation 2000).

Other forms of philanthropy continue to be important. Local gifts of land have steadily added substantial acreage to the state parks system since the first decades of the twentieth century. Figure 32 shows that these acreages, and their dollar values, have increased over the years.

Land use watchdogs also strive to build capacity among local government and nongovernmental organizations. The San Francisco Bay Area's Greenbelt Alliance has long published extensive guides to land use re-

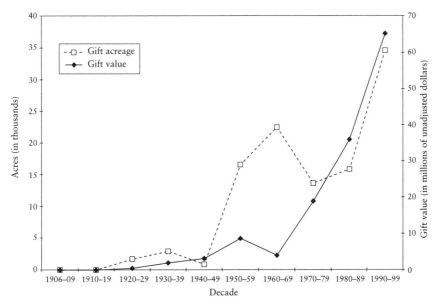

Figure 32. Gifts to the California State Parks and Recreation Department, by decade.

forms, with titles like "A Citizen's Guide to Using Urban Growth Boundaries" or "Strategies for Bay Area Greenspace Groups" (Greenbelt Alliance 2000). Says Mark Green, executive director of Conservation Action in Sonoma County:

> We've worked closely with Greenbelt Alliance. The press referred to us as the "potent one-two punch" for the county's environmental movement. Greenbelt Alliance is, of course, a regional organization that works all over the Bay Area. Because we have this extraordinary political organizing tool, we have been able to knock on every door of every city in Sonoma County, at least once, talking with people about what an urban growth boundary is and encouraging . . . passage [of such a boundary] for that local community. As of now, all but three of the cities in Sonoma County have approved voter-approved urban growth boundaries that set a line beyond which the city is not allowed to extend its services for twenty years.

The GreenInfo Network is another nongovernmental organization that fosters technical expertise in Northern California by providing "computer based mapping to non-profits, public agencies and other public interest organizations" (GreenInfo Network 2000).

Capacity building evolves hand-in-hand with collaboration. Because so many land preservation deals require multiple funders, agencies, or trusts, the staffs of public and private organizations come to know each other well. Larger, older organizations learn of the strengths and short-comings of smaller, newer agencies or nongovernmental organizations and thus become uniquely poised to provide assistance effectively.

A positive record of collaboration also changes the kinds of preserva-tion programs public and private organizations undertake today. For instance, instead of usually shouldering large acquisitions on its own, the Nature Conservancy has become more willing to acquire small pieces of important ecoregions in some parts of the state, because local landown-ers, small trusts, and state and local agencies have demonstrated com-mitment to a common preservation agenda. Some trusts have taken their collaboration with public agencies to a new level, as the director of a land trust on the Central Coast made clear:

> I think one of the most important functions a land trust fills for the public is to acquire a land bank for public agencies. . . . That's a role a land trust can really fill to bridge the gap between public and private sectors, . . . [It takes] over the management until the public agency is ready to take it on. And I see that happening more and more.

Finally, the budget crisis facing land preservationists throughout the state politicized even the most staid land trusts, who mounted vigorous campaigns on behalf of Propositions 12 and 13 (the park and water bonds) in the fall and winter of 2000. Of the $8.2 million dollars spent on Propositions 12 and 13, $2.1 million was contributed by the Nature Conservancy and another $680,000 was contributed by other private land trusts—or about 35 percent of all donations (California Secretary of State 2000).[7] In contrast, on the previous park bond that passed— Proposition 70 in 1988—land trusts spent about $168,000, or 23 per-cent of total spending on that measure. In 1988, TNC contributed less than 2 percent of the total funds raised for Proposition 70; in 2000, TNC's share of donations was 26 percent (ibid.; California Fair Political Practices Commission 1988).

TNC even conducted its own polls on the propositions, and then shared its findings with campaign strategists and supportive legislators. The fiscal imperative—raise money for the state parks and local agencies or shoulder the preservation burden alone—prompted TPL, TNC, and many others to break their carefully cultivated silence and political neutrality.

POLICY REFORMS

Preservationists, organizations, and policy makers at all levels can take steps to cultivate environmental policy capacity throughout the state. Not all aspects of policy capacity are likely to respond to concerted policy interventions; for example, it is hard to imagine civic environmentalism blossoming as a result of some sort of social engineering program orchestrated by the state or federal government. Nonetheless, policy makers and activists alike can do much more than they are doing currently.

Policy reforms that would improve the possibility of land preservation can be grouped by the different aspects of policy capacity they address. First, the state and federal governments can alter the fiscal incentives that public and private actors face, motivating them to choose preservation over development more often. Even the administrative capacity of local institutions can and should be developed with help from both the public and private sectors. Second, states can make it much easier for local governments to coordinate their planning and manage growth with a regional—as opposed to a more parochial and municipal—scope. Third, communities and states must create some new institutions to protect and manage open space.

Improving Fiscal Resources

By the late 1990s, California's fiscal crisis seemed to be over. The state was running a budget surplus; voters passed record school, park, and water bonds at the statewide level; and unemployment was lower than ever. Unfortunately for preservationists, the booming economy brought not only rapid development and growth, but also soaring land prices. As a result, the record sums spent on land preservation in the last few years of the century did not buy appreciably more acres; instead, preservationists made modest gains, always protecting only a few acres for the many that were taken out of farm production and other open space.

In this economic expansion, keeping up with farmland conversion and development would require preserving, absorbing, and managing at least 50,000 new acres per year, right at the urban edges. At a conservatively estimated cost of $10,000 per acre, that amounts to $500 million per year. This figure is substantially more than the total acquisition budget for local open space, counting all funding sources, in the year 2000. Although it is difficult to get an exact count, these sources combined spent about

$200 million in 2000 on direct land acquisition at the local level; funders
include the state Department of Parks and Recreation (using park bond
funds), the federal government (using Land and Water Conservation Fund
monies), special recreation and parks districts, other local government parks
agencies (using either development fees and exactions, property taxes, or
general revenues), the state's land trusts, the Packard Foundation, the
Nature Conservancy, and the Trust for Public Land. Even in the strongest
economy, the costs of preservation would exceed available budgets.

An increase in local budgets for open space can occur in four ways.
First, local governments across the country, not just in California, need
expanded powers, incentives, and political will to pass "adequate public
facilities ordinances," which are essentially development exactions for
infrastructure. The construction industry's protestations notwithstanding,
new development creates greater direct and indirect costs than the benefits
it confers in property and sales taxes. An added benefit of raising development fees is that subsequent projects tend to be more compact, thereby
more efficiently using new urban space (Pendall 1999). California's
Quimby Act, which allows cities and counties to exact park acquisition
and development fees from developers, is quite restrictive and limited in
scope. Broadening the formulas so that local government could tailor its
development impact fees to regional needs would go a long way toward
making the act useful in today's land preservation context.

Second, private philanthropy could do much more to equalize the
benefits of land trust activity around the state. Preservationists applaud
the generosity of the Packard Foundation and the larger land trusts who
are the most successful fund-raisers, but the benefits conferred by these
organizations tend to be concentrated in just a few counties.

Third, the state can commit a larger part of its general revenues to various land preservation programs and thereby equalize preservation activities across counties and cities. An Orange County planner stressed the
role of the state in opposing anti-environmental parochialism: "I've seen
some times where we really needed the environmentally sensitive assembly members and state senators from Northern California and other
parts of the southland to help us protect what we have here against the
greediness of local politicians, many of whom are kind of antigovernment, and antipark, and this kind of thing—you know, pro-business."
California can support farmland preservation much more aggressively by
increasing its funding of the California Farmland Conservancy Program
(formerly called the Agricultural Land Stewardship Program), which
makes funds available to purchase agricultural conservation easements.

Fourth, and by far the most difficult to achieve, states and local governments need the authority to raise local revenues with simple instead of two-thirds majorities. Fourteen states require their legislatures and/or local governments to win the approval of a supermajority of voters in order to increase taxes.[8] The antitax legacy of the 1970s sharply constrains local budgets even in the best economic times. State legislators in California attempted to reduce the constitutional requirement that two-thirds of voters must approve local school bonds (down to a simple majority) in March 2000, but their measure, Proposition 26, failed by about 2.5 percent. Another statewide ballot measure reducing the approval requirement for local school bonds from two-thirds to 55 percent passed on the November 2000 ballot (Proposition 39). Strategists viewed these efforts at easing the approval requirements for school bonds as litmus tests for other issues; for example, if voters would not lower approval requirements for schools, how could campaign organizers hope to lower local approval requirements for transportation infrastructure or parks? The success with Proposition 39 provided reason for cautious optimism.

The Paradox of Development and the Urgency for Regional Planning

One of the most common ways to preserve land is to keep development out by imposing growth controls, which are usually city or county ordinances limiting the number of new residential or commercial units that can be built per year. Although dozens of such measures have been placed on local ballots and passed by California's voters, several studies question whether they are effective at halting or slowing sprawl, much less at preserving open space.

In a thorough study of growth-control ordinances passed in the San Francisco Bay Area in the 1980s, Q. Shen found that "ordinances that impose limits on the rate or amount of population growth or residential development have effectively restricted housing supply within the jurisdictional areas" (1996, p. 86). Shen goes on to point out that growth simply shifts to parts of the region that do not have growth controls, and that wealthier cities absorbed less population growth in the 1980s than would be expected. R. Pendall echoed Shen's findings: "The spatial effects of land-use controls depend probably on the type of control. Zoning for large lots, limiting issuance of building permits, and establishing moratoria on development . . . can limit the supply of new housing in the jurisdictions that impose them" (1999, p. 557). John D. Landis (1992) and Christopher Leo and colleagues (1998) also support the notion that growth controls fail because they do not change the essentially regional problems of balancing new job creation with housing stock, offsetting the infrastructure costs associated with new developments (and more generally, providing counties with enough funds to meet their social services mandates), and rationalizing transportation infrastructure.

Land preservation does not always prevent sprawl, for the same reasons that growth controls fail. An aggressive, restrictive greenbelt around one city may encourage development to leapfrog into the next receptive community. Regional growth management could go a long way toward addressing development pressures, and states like Florida and Oregon have given themselves broad powers to induce growth management, thereby creating more compact development. Oregon goes so far as to deny building permits if development plans are not in line with state guidelines (Nelson 1999).

But such an approach requires vigorous, sustained state leadership aimed at rationalizing regional land use, an essentially unheard-of phenomenon in California (Leo et al. 1998; Pincetl 1999), and thus it is more likely to occur in states like Oregon or Minnesota. California has a long history of flirting with regional forms of governance; most of the agencies that have resulted have ended up in the dustbin or emerged as advisory and analytic bodies rather than institutions with real land use powers (Press 1995).

In counties that have multiple slow-growth communities in relatively close proximity, essentially local efforts can be effective. As Pendall puts it, "Local governments . . . can identify areas where higher densities are appropriate, create incentives for high-density development to occur there, and work in voluntary councils of government to coordinate land use policies with neighboring jurisdictions. They can encourage redevelopment of underused and abandoned properties, identify locally owned tax-delinquent properties for rehabilitation and occupancy, and provide additional opportunities for mixed uses in urban and suburban neighborhoods" (1999, p. 570). However the details may vary, effective regional growth management requires leadership by the state. Substantively, a regional approach must not only set some multijurisdiction cap on growth but must also offset infrastructure costs through taxes or exactions (Leo et al. 1998). And as the planned growth advocates of the 1980s argued, "no growth at all" is not a realistic alternative in any region or state whose job creation outstrips its housing stock by ratios of two-to-one or more. Consequently, those regional and state-led growth management programs that clearly permit infill development and new housing in appropriate zones encounter much less opposition from developers while satisfying demand (Leo et al. 1998; Nelson 1999).[9]

States can take even small steps toward regional growth management by requiring local jurisdictions to assess the consequences of proposed developments much more thoroughly. The California legislature attempted to do so with AB 1277 in the 1999–2000 session, which would have required Local Agency Formation Commissions—the county agencies that permit cities to expand their boundaries—to assess the water supply implications of new annexations, but the bill died in committee. If cities and counties could quantify the dollar cost of new development—for infrastructure, transportation, open space—using formulas broadly defined by the state, local government could then draw on uniform and comprehensive structures for development impact fees.

In the 1990s, the federal government got into the business of growth management at the level of exhortation, encouragement, and research. The EPA, for years a pollution control agency, developed extensive programmatic depth in land use under the rubrics "smart growth" and "livable communities." These programs merged new technical assistance with old regulatory efforts in areas such as brownfields redevelopment, watershed protection (with development controls), and transportation planning, to cite a few (US EPA 2001). Smart growth also became a programmatic element in the federal Department of Interior (US DOI 2001) and Department of Transportation (US DOT 2001a).

Throughout the 1960s and 1970s, when federal monies flowed to states and communities for important acquisitions, the government demonstrated the important role it can play in land preservation. Smart growth and "livable communities" programs will work if they essentially change the federal government's role, from that of reluctant funder of last resort to active, frequent collaborator. State and federal agencies would lessen communities' preservation responsibilities by concentrating on large purchases close to urban centers, which tend to be expensive but highly popular, and on crucial parcels for protection of biodiversity. For example, the U.S. Fish and Wildlife Service budgeted $68 million for local habitat acquisition efforts in 2001. While this news was good for California, which received almost half the total sum, the remaining $40 million was far too little to make much of a difference nationwide.

Regardless of which agencies or institutions adopt growth controls, such policies tend to be reactive. As development occurs, governments can raise fees or land dedications on behalf of land preservation, which points to an ironic peculiarity of the growth machine: in some parts of the state, preservation paradoxically relies on the construction industry to directly provide open space lands or the necessary funds for protecting land.

Some may seize upon this paradox to conclude that development is a necessary (or sufficient) condition for preservation, but it would be a mistake to do so, for several reasons. First, development itself generates a relatively small budget for land preservation, and many construction projects do not contribute to protection at all. In densely urbanized areas, even the highest development impact fees purchase only postage-stamp-size parks—larger parcels are too expensive or simply not available. However, development *pressure* or even the perception of rapid growth motivates many preservation projects in California's exurban areas. Moreover, residents of one county may become proactive as they perceive growing pressure in neighboring counties. Second, most successful land preservation entrepreneurs uncouple development from land acquisition and protection. Land trusts, foundations, and open space agencies pursue large regional or watershed-level land acquisition programs well in advance of changes in zoning (e.g., from agricultural to residential or commercial) or rising land values.

Creating New Institutions

Containing development, slowing growth, and assessing the impacts of new construction can all help keep undeveloped land as open space and agricultural land, but they do little to actually acquire such lands. For some communities, infusions of funds will not move land acquisition forward much, because such jurisdictions lack the institutional capacity to absorb and manage new lands.

The experiences of counties like Santa Clara and Sonoma suggest that new open space districts and land trusts will be needed in the Sierra foothills, the southern Central Coast, the Central Valley, and urbanizing rural regions around the country. The state legislature creates new public open space districts, usually when local leaders and the public show overwhelming support and need for such new agencies. In late 2000, one such effort was under way in Santa Barbara County, led by a Santa Barbara city councilwoman, a land trust director, a county supervisor, a developer, a planning commissioner, and the local legislative representatives (Green 2000).

In other communities, such as those in the tax-shy Central Valley, a state conservancy approach may be more viable. With local support, the state can create regional conservancies that act very much like open space districts but enjoy permanent funding in the state budget.

The wave of city annexations and incorporations will not stop, but for some communities, incorporating a new city may signal that locals are trying to wrest control of their land use decisions from a pro-growth county government, rather than attempting to grow faster. This was the case with the Sonoma County town of Windsor. A town council member pointed out that, while the town had existed for 150 years, "it has doubled its population in the last seven [years]; it was 8,000 people in 1987 or '86 when it was really starting to grow, and now it's 20,000. And a lot of the growth was between '88, '89, '90, '91; and that's why Windsor became a town. . . . One of the reasons was because we voted to incorporate so we could have control over our growth."

Civic Environmentalism

Although not a *public* policy reform, encouraging the spread of civic environmentalism is a critical element for cultivating and sustaining future environmental policy capacity. Environmental nongovernmental organizations, schools, and the nationwide adopt-a-creek movement surely help in that direction, as do some of the country's philanthropic foundations. However, we tend to be limited in the kinds of landscapes we celebrate, overlooking our farm and valley communities as merely places to drive through on our way to someplace else. Encouraging widespread civic environmentalism will require that more educators and preservationists cultivate place attachments in the communities historically left behind by open space advocates.

Civic environmentalism is at its strongest when people can use it to exercise *both* negative and positive authority. It is rarely enough to simply keep the bulldozers at bay (negative authority) by using, for instance, the Not-in-My-Back-Yard tactics so effective around the country. The land scrapers will return. The challenge for the grassroots as well as for elite entrepreneurs is to mobilize local communities not just to address problems but also to make appealing visions a reality before problems are upon them.

. . .

Most of all we need a vision, an ideal of what the state can be—a land that
would permit the greatest diversity of human activities and the fullest ex-
pression of human freedom in a setting of natural splendor and man-made
beauty.

Ray Dasmann, *The Destruction of California*

When Ray Dasmann wrote *The Destruction of California* in 1965, he
could point to a great number of planners and agency officials attempting more or less independently to manage California's landscapes somewhat sustainably. While much of what Dasmann urged us to preserve has
disappeared in the intervening years, we have also learned a great deal
and formed enduring institutions to carry out a preservationist vision.
We have information and technical know-how in the form of policy
innovations and GIS programs, and we have expertise in the ways of running and funding preservation campaigns. But the state as a whole list-
lessly makes use of its environmental policy capacity. It is as if we had the
legs of a marathon runner but used them only to walk around the block.
The political timidity displayed in Sacramento—even when the economy
could not have been better—mirrors a profound reluctance to mess with
private enterprise and property rights.

This reluctance is understandable, given the bruising the public sector
took in the years since President Jimmy Carter's administration. The
antitax crusade, federal court rulings in favor of property rights advocates, the vitriol of the Wise Use Movement, the punishment that elected
officials suffered for attempts to regulate industry—all conspired to close
many of the state's policy windows.

Local land preservation provides a timely opportunity for policy makers to shed their decades-long political timidity. First, there is an unusu-
ally close relationship between policy outputs and outcomes in the land
preservation arena. Most of the time, acquisition dollars unambiguously
beget land preservation. Second, the returns on land preservation policies
are ongoing and will far outstrip initial investments. Third, keeping land
in open space maintains the state's options, whether these consist of
efforts to create new recreation areas or to allow habitats to adapt as climate change progresses (Field et al. 1999). Finally, land preservation
pursued with essentially local policy capacity ultimately affirms the twin
promises of sustainability and democracy. The landscapes themselves
confirm for their communities that democracy can work for nature and
people.

Acres of Land Held in Fee Simple by Local Government and Land Trusts, by County

County	Government City	County	Special district	Local gifts to California state parks	Land trusts[a]
Alameda	5,203	231	51,641	0	1,610
Amador	13	634	0	0	952
Butte	0	0	3,062	225	265
Calaveras	0	0	0	40	2,830
Colusa	0	0	0	16	1,152
Contra Costa	5,543	68	40,735	2,422	2,663
El Dorado	2,058	2,721	434	167	2,588
Fresno	1,564	1,052	103	0	4,551
Glenn	74	0	0	0	0
Humboldt	1,014	1,028	203	20,141	91,857
Imperial	162	1,339	0	0	0
Kern	265	3,091	439	163	94,445
Kings	243	0	0	0	0
Lake	55	0	0	334	2,061
Lassen	107	1,142	0	0	641
Los Angeles	34,042	65,928	0	1,992	48,655
Madera	56	0	0	2	0
Marin	2,563	2,543	14,883	302	27,510
Mendocino	3,251	545	47	1,544	15,120
Merced	240	810	0	10	7,100
Monterey	1,373	14,799	5,670	3,003	37,867

County	Government		Special district	Local gifts to California state parks	Land trusts[a]
	City	County			
Napa	815	0	0	83	12,961
Nevada	0	92	80	15	1,510
Orange	7,148	22,029	191	63	1,241
Placer	679	309	233	<1	145
Riverside	5,266	21,787	222	11,576	25,327
Sacramento	2,265	11,496	1,260	560	241
San Benito	0	145	0	1	1,768
San Bernardino	7,649	8,477	889	41	35,689
San Diego	26,263	13,295	1,185	7,615	29,354
San Francisco	2,959	0	0	29	0
San Joaquin	991	614	0	<1	6,284
San Luis Obispo	9,413	2,337	4,276	1,109	538
San Mateo	2,187	13,834	15,714	2,773	36,996
Santa Barbara	2,071	2,455	49	20	3,328
Santa Clara	9,282	38,963	28,120	12,356	2,607
Santa Cruz	1,810	1,282	471	19,913	20,073
Shasta	537	130	0	1,094	0
Solano	15,117	448	0	89	4,942
Sonoma	1,827	4,113	472	600	14,701
Stanislaus	1,338	9,462	0	0	0
Sutter	45	0	0	0	200
Tehama	97	126	0	0	0
Tulare	1,044	608	0	<1	941
Ventura	1,181	5,816	7,507	136	20
Yolo	434	1,159	13	0	810
Yuba	267	255	0	0	10

NOTE: Excludes water-district and flood-control-district holdings and parcels that are fewer than 10 acres in the above counties. The table also excludes the counties of Alpine, Del Norte, Inyo, Mariposa, Modoc, Mono, Plumas, Sierra, Siskiyou, Trinity, and Tuolumne.

[a] Fee simple ownership, easements, and transfers.

The Community and Conservation in California Survey Questionnaire

1. First, how long have you lived in your county? (Round to the nearest year.)

   1 = [Number of years]
   0 = Less than one year
   8 = Don't know
   9 = Refused

2. Have you always lived in the area you live in now?

   1 = Yes
   2 = No
   8 = Don't know
   9 = Refused

3a. How did you come to live in the area where you live now? (Enter "1" for each item selected.)

   a. Grew up there
   b. To take a job in this area, or for spouse to take a job
   c. To get an education, then stayed
   d. To be close to family
   e. Because this is the kind of place I wanted to live

   What about it in particular made it the kind of place you wanted to live in?

   f. Scenic area
   g. Comfortable with the values of people who live in this area.
   h. Clean environment—water, air
   i. Safe, low crime

     j. To get away from big-city problems
     k. To find affordable housing
     l. Retired here
     m. Be close to friends
     n. Other, please specify

3b. Regardless of why you came to live in your area, I'd like you to tell me whether the following items are very important to you, somewhat important, or not at all important as part of your attachment to the place where you live.

     1 = Very important
     2 = Somewhat important
     3 = Not at all important
     8 = Don't know
     9 = Refused

     a. Close to relatives or in-laws
     b. Friends live nearby
     c. People are very friendly here
     d. It's close to your job
     e. Affordable housing
     f. Scenic area
     g. Clean environment
     h. Safe area
     i. Strong schools
     j. University or college nearby
     k. Medical services available nearby
     l. Good civic leadership
     m. Low property taxes
     n. Can't afford to leave
     o. You take care of aging relatives here
     p. Small town lifestyle
     q. Weather or climate
     r. Recreational opportunities
     z. Any other reason?
     s. How important is this reason?

4. Do you expect to stay in the area where you live now?

     1 = Yes
     2 = No (go to v6)
     8 = Don't know
     9 = Refused

5. Do you expect to live there . . .

     1 = A very long time—10 to 15 years or more
     2 = A long time—5 to 9 years
     3 = A few more years—2 to 4 years
     4 = A short time—less than 2 years

8 = Don't know
9 = Refused

6. How would you feel if you had to move away from the area where you live now? Would you be . . .

1 = Very sorry to leave
2 = Somewhat sorry to leave
3 = Somewhat pleased to leave
4 = Very pleased to leave or
5 = Would you not care one way or the other
8 = Don't know
9 = Refused

7then. Was the area where you previously lived urban, suburban, or rural? (If v2 = 2, go to v7 now)

1 = Urban
2 = Suburban
3 = Rural
8 = Don't know
9 = Refused

7now. Is the area where you live now urban, suburban, or rural?

1 = Urban
2 = Suburban
3 = Rural
8 = Don't know
9 = Refused

8. Comparing the environmental quality (e.g., pollution and physical beauty of the surroundings) of the area where you previously lived with the area you live in now, would you say the environmental quality of the area where you live now is . . . (If v2 = 2, go to v9)

1 = Substantially better
2 = Somewhat better
3 = About the same
4 = Somewhat worse
5 = Substantially worse
8 = Don't know
9 = Refused

9. Please rate the following government services in the place where you live as being excellent, good, fair, or poor.

1 = Excellent
2 = Good
3 = Fair
4 = Poor
8 = Don't know
9 = Refused

a. Police protection
b. Water
c. Fire protection
d. Garbage collection
e. Emergency response service
f. Child care services
g. Senior citizen services
h. Programs for youth
i. Street cleaning
j. Street repair
k. Upkeep of parks
l. Number of parks

10. Next, I will mention some things that may or may not be a problem where you live. For each one, please tell me if you think it is a problem where you live.

   1 = Yes, it is a problem
   2 = No, it is not a problem
   8 = Don't know
   9 = Refused

   a. Lack of jobs
   b. Quality of schools
   c. Too much crime
   d. Too much traffic
   e. Air pollution
   f. Loss of family farms
   g. Development of hillsides, wetlands, or other natural areas
   h. Closing of small businesses
   i. Housing costs
   j. Lack of leadership
   k. Loss of community spirit
   l. People moving out of town
   m. People moving into town

11. Is it a major problem or a minor problem?

   1 = Major problem
   2 = Minor problem
   8 = Don't know
   9 = Refused

12. About what proportion of your adult relatives and in-laws, other than very distantly related persons, live within a couple hours' drive from your home?

   1 = I have no living relatives or in-laws
   2 = None of them
   3 = Less than one-half of them

4 = About one-half of them
5 = Most of them
6 = All of them
8 = Don't know
9 = Refused

13. About what proportion of all your close personal adult friends live within a couple hours' drive from your home?

1 = I really have no close personal friends
2 = None of them
3 = Less than one-half of them
4 = About one-half of them
5 = Most of them
6 = All of them
8 = Don't know
9 = Refused

14. About what proportion of your neighbors would you say you know by name?

1 = None or very few
2 = Less than half of them
3 = About half of them
4 = Most of them
5 = All of them
8 = Don't know
9 = Refused

15. Some people care a lot about feeling part of their neighborhood or community. For others, this is not so important. How important is it to you to feel part of your neighborhood or community?

1 = Very important
2 = Somewhat important
3 = Slightly important or
4 = Not at all important
8 = Don't know
9 = Refused

16. How important are parks that maintain open space, with hiking trails, nature preserves, or campgrounds; would you say they are very important, somewhat important, slightly important, or not at all important?

1 = Very important
2 = Somewhat important
3 = Slightly important
4 = Not at all important
8 = Don't know
9 = Refused

17. How about parks with things such as little league baseball fields, playgrounds, tennis courts, or picnic areas; would you say that these types of parks are very important, somewhat important, slightly important, or not at all important?

    1 = Very important
    2 = Somewhat important
    3 = Slightly important
    4 = Not at all important
    8 = Don't know
    9 = Refused

18. On average, how many times per month do you visit public parks or open space?

    (If 0, go to v20)

    Times per month

19. About how long does it take you to drive to your favorite park or open space areas?

    Hour(s) and minutes

20. Are you aware of any activity or publicity in your community around issues regarding the acquisition, development, or maintenance of open space or parklands?

    1 = Yes
    2 = No
    9 = Refused

21. Are you familiar with land trusts (nonprofit organizations that purchase land to preserve it)?

    1 = Yes
    2 = No
    9 = Refused

22. How did you learn about land trusts? (Enter "1" for each item selected.)

    22@1 TV
    22@2 Radio
    22@3 Magazine/book
    22@4 Newspaper
    22@5 Environmental organization
    22@6 Friend/relative
    22@7 Other

23. One way citizens can purchase and maintain open space is to create a special assessment district for that purpose. In such a special district, each residential-property owner pays a certain amount each year into a fund to buy and preserve open space. If an annual tax were brought to a vote in your area, how much additional

money would you be willing to pay each year in order to buy and preserve open space?

1 = $0 (Skip to v24a)
2 = $1–$10
3 = $11–$20
4 = $21–$30
5 = $31–$40
6 = $41–$50
7 = $51 or more
8 = Don't know
9 = Refused

24. Why would you favor this proposal? (Enter "1" for each item selected.)

24@1 Preserve/protect open space
24@2 It's important to have open space
24@3 Not much open space left
24@4 Need for recreation and/or parks
24@5 Need to control growth/development
24@6 Control population/congestion
24@7 Important for quality of life
24@8 Protect wildlife/nature
24@9 For future/future generations
24@10 Need for pollution control
24@11 Like it/it's a good idea
24@12 Other, please specify
24@13 Important to preserve agricultural land

24a. Why would you oppose this proposal? (Enter "1" for each item selected.)

24a1 Don't want any more taxes
24a2 Too much money
24a3 More money for government to waste
24a4 Money will be mismanaged
24a5 Need more development
24a6 Development is good for jobs/economy
24a7 Need more homes
24a8 No confidence in elected board or officials
24a9 Enough open space/Don't need more
24a10 Don't need it/Bad idea
24a11 Other, please specify

25. Would you support a state tax bond measure if it were proposed as a way to fund the acquisition, development, and maintenance of California state parklands?

1 = Yes
2 = No

8 = Don't know
9 = Refused

26. Are you currently employed, unemployed, retired, a homemaker, or a student?

    1 = Employed, including self-employed
    2 = Unemployed, including laid off
    3 = Retired
    4 = Homemaker
    5 = Student
    6 = Disabled
    7 = Other
    8 = Don't know
    9 = Refused

    (2–4, 6 skip to v28kids)

27. Do you work as well as go to school?

    1 = Yes
    2 = No

28. On average, how many hours a week do you work?

    Number of hours:

28kids. Do you currently have children under the age of eighteen living at home?

    1 = Yes
    2 = No
    8 = Don't know
    9 = Refused

29. I'm going to read a list of activities; please tell me whether you have spent time participating in each of them in the past year.

29a. What about taking continuing or adult education classes— have you done this in the past year?

    1 = Yes
    2 = No
    8 = Don't know
    9 = Refused

29b. What about exercising or working out—have you done this in the past year?

    1 = Yes
    2 = No
    8 = Don't know
    9 = Refused

29c. What about attending a self-help group, such as groups to help you lose weight, quit smoking, or make other personal improvements?

1 = Yes
2 = No
8 = Don't know
9 = Refused

29d. What about attending church or religious services?

1 = Yes
2 = No
8 = Don't know
9 = Refused

29e. What about participating in a reading group, religious study group, or other study group?

1 = Yes
2 = No
8 = Don't know
9 = Refused

29f. What about participating in organized recreational leagues, such as softball or bowling leagues?

1 = Yes
2 = No
8 = Don't know
9 = Refused

29g. What about playing cards or board games with a usual group of friends?

1 = Yes
2 = No
8 = Don't know
9 = Refused

29h. What about using a computer to send or receive personal e-mail or to get involved in on-line discussions or "chat groups" over the Internet?

1 = Yes
2 = No
8 = Don't know
9 = Refused

29i. What about participating in an organized playgroup?

1 = Yes
2 = No
8 = Don't know
9 = Refused

29num. In the past month, how many times have you done this?

  a–i. Times per month
  8 = Don't know
  9 = Refused

30. Next I would like to ask you about volunteer activity. By volunteer activity I mean spending time helping without being paid for it.

30a. In the past year have you volunteered your time to any church or religious group?

  1 = Yes
  2 = No
  8 = Don't know
  9 = Refused

30b. In the past year have you volunteered your time to any political organizations or candidates?

  1 = Yes
  2 = No
  8 = Don't know
  9 = Refused

30c. In the past year have you volunteered your time to any school or tutoring program?

  1 = Yes
  2 = No
  8 = Don't know
  9 = Refused

30d. In the past year have you volunteered your time to any adopt-a-creek, -beach, -highway, -park activities?

  1 = Yes
  2 = No
  8 = Don't know
  9 = Refused

30e. In the past year have you volunteered your time to any other environmental organization?

  1 = Yes
  2 = No
  8 = Don't know
  9 = Refused

30f. In the past year have you volunteered your time to any child or youth development programs, such as day care centers, scouts, or Little League?

  1 = Yes
  2 = No

8 = Don't know

9 = Refused

30g. In the past year have you volunteered your time to any arts or cultural organizations, like a theater or music group, museum, or public TV station?

1 = Yes

2 = No

8 = Don't know

9 = Refused

30h. In the past year have you volunteered your time to any hospital or health organization, including those that fight particular diseases?

1 = Yes

2 = No

8 = Don't know

9 = Refused

30i. In the past year have you volunteered your time to any local government boards or commissions?

1 = Yes

2 = No

8 = Don't know

9 = Refused

30j. In the past year have you volunteered your time to any neighborhood, civic or community group, such as a block association or neighborhood watch?

1 = Yes

2 = No

8 = Don't know

9 = Refused

30k. In the past year have you volunteered your time to any organization to help the poor, elderly, or homeless?

1 = Yes

2 = No

8 = Don't know

9 = Refused

30l. In the past year have you volunteered your time to give blood?

1 = Yes

2 = No

8 = Don't know

9 = Refused

30m. In the past year have you volunteered your time to other one-time or ad hoc community work?

1 = Yes

2 = No
8 = Don't know
9 = Refused

30n.   In the past year have you volunteered your time to help after a nat-
       ural disaster (e.g., flood, wildfire, or earthquake)?

       1 = Yes
       2 = No
       8 = Don't know
       9 = Refused

30num. In the past month, on about how many days, if any, have you done
       this?

       a–n Days per month
       8 = Don't know
       9 = Refused

30oth. And when you volunteered did you primarily work with others or
       alone?

       1 = Mostly worked with others
       2 = Mostly worked alone
       8 = Don't know
       9 = Refused

31a.   What keeps you from volunteering in these kinds of activities?

       1 = Did not have the time
       2 = Did not want to
       3 = No one asked you to help
       4 = Did not have the opportunity
       5 = Health problems
       8 = Don't know
       9 = Refused

31b.   What keeps you from volunteering more in these kinds of activities?

       1 = Did not have the time
       2 = Did not want to
       3 = No one asked you to help
       4 = Did not have the opportunity
       5 = Health problems
       8 = Don't know
       9 = Refused

32x.   In the past year, which of the following positions have you held
       in a voluntary group or organization? (Enter "1" for each item
       selected.)

       32@1 None
       32@2 Member
       32@3 Special project coordinator

32@4 Board member
32@5 Executive position (president, secretary, etc.)

33. I have one more short list of community activities. As I read each one, please tell me if you have ever done it.

33a. Have you ever attended a town meeting, public hearing, or public affairs discussion group?

1 = Yes
2 = No
8 = Don't know
9 = Refused

33b. Have you ever called, sent a letter, e-mailed, or faxed any elected official?

1 = Yes
2 = No
8 = Don't know
9 = Refused

33c. Have you ever joined or contributed money to an organization in support of a particular cause?

1 = Yes
2 = No
8 = Don't know
9 = Refused

33d. Have you ever participated in union activities?

1 = Yes
2 = No
8 = Don't know
9 = Refused

33e. Have you ever joined together with coworkers to solve a workplace problem?

1 = Yes
2 = No
8 = Don't know
9 = Refused

33num. In the past year, about how many times have you done this?

a–e Times per year
8 = Don't know
9 = Refused

34ax. Were these meetings with officials an effort to get your local government to do something about some needs or problems that concerned you? If yes, have you done this more than once?

1 = Yes, tried once

2 = Yes, tried more than once
3 = No
8 = Don't know
9 = Refused
(If 1 go to v34aa; if 2 go to v34ba)

34bx. Were these contacts with officials an effort to get your local government to do something about some needs or problems that concerned you? If yes, have you done this more than once?

1 = Yes, tried once
2 = Yes, tried more than once
3 = No
8 = Don't know
9 = Refused
(If 1 go to v34ab; if 2 go to v34bb)

34aa. Was this need or problem primarily of concern to you, your friends and family, or was it an issue of wider concern?

1 = Self, friends or family
2 = Both
3 = Wider concern
8 = Don't know
9 = Refused

34ab. Was this need or problem primarily of concern to you, your friends and family, or was it an issue of wider concern?

1 = Self, friends, or family
2 = Both
3 = Wider concern
8 = Don't know
9 = Refused

34ba. Were these needs or problems primarily of concern to you, your friends and family, or were they issues of wider concern?

1 = Self, friends or family
2 = Both
3 = Wider concern
8 = Don't know
9 = Refused

34bb. Were these needs or problems primarily of concern to you, your friends and family, or were they issues of wider concern?

1 = Self, friends, or family
2 = Both
3 = Wider concern
8 = Don't know
9 = Refused

35a. Were you successful in getting local government to do what you wanted?

1 = Yes
2 = No
3 = Sometimes/Depends
8 = Don't know
9 = Refused

35b. Were you successful in getting local government to do what you wanted?

1 = Yes
2 = No
3 = Sometimes/Depends
8 = Don't know
9 = Refused

36. The next question is about government services and spending in general. Which do you think would be best: for government to reduce spending and provide fewer services, to continue the services it now provides even if that means no reduction in spending, or to provide more services even if that means increased spending?

1 = Provide fewer services to reduce spending
2 = Continue services it now provides
3 = Provide more services even if it means an increase in spending
8 = Don't know
9 = Refused

37. What do you think is most important in your area: to promote private development even if it means loss of some open space, or regulate development to protect open space, or do you think the balance between regulation and development is about right in your area?

1 = Promote private development
2 = Regulate private development
3 = Neither promote or regulate—balance is about right now
8 = Don't know
9 = Refused

38. How would you rate the economy in your area now? Would you say it's very good, good, fair, or poor?

1 = Very good
2 = Good
3 = Fair
4 = Poor
8 = Don't know
9 = Refused

39. Would you say your family's income depends a great deal, somewhat, not very much, or not at all on private economic development in your area?

    1 = A great deal
    2 = Somewhat
    3 = Not very much
    4 = Not at all
    8 = Don't know
    9 = Refused

40. Are you currently registered to vote?

    1 = Yes/Don't have to register
    2 = No
    8 = Don't know
    9 = Refused

41. Did you vote in the 1996 presidential election?

    1 = Yes
    2 = No
    8 = Don't know
    9 = Refused

42. How often do you vote in local elections (in your county, city, or
town)?

    1 = Every time
    2 = Almost every time
    3 = Sometimes
    4 = Hardly ever
    5 = Never
    8 = Don't know
    9 = Refused

43. Next I would like to ask you a few questions about trust. Generally speaking, would you say that most people can be trusted?

    1 = Yes
    2 = No
    3 = Depends
    8 = Don't know
    9 = Refused

44. Generally speaking, do you think that most people who come into
contact with you trust you?

    1 = Yes, most people trust me
    2 = No, people are suspicious of me
    3 = Depends
    8 = Don't know
    9 = Refused

45. In general, do you think it is easier or harder to trust a person about the same age as yourself?

   1 = Easier
   2 = Harder
   3 = Age doesn't matter
   8 = Don't know
   9 = Refused
   (If 1 go to v45eas; if 2 go to v45hard)

45eas. Do you think it is easier to trust people who are younger than you or older than you?

   1 = Younger
   2 = Older
   3 = Both
   8 = Don't know
   9 = Refused

45hard. Do you think it is harder to trust people who are younger than you or older than you?

   1 = Younger
   2 = Older
   3 = Both
   8 = Don't know
   9 = Refused

46a. In general, do you think it's easier to trust a man or a woman?

   1 = Man
   2 = Woman
   3 = Sex doesn't matter
   8 = Don't know
   9 = Refused

46b. In general, do you think it's easier to trust a woman or a man?

   1 = Man
   2 = Woman
   3 = Sex doesn't matter
   8 = Don't know
   9 = Refused

47. In general, do you think it's easier or harder to trust a person of a different race from yourself?

   1 = Easier
   2 = Harder
   3 = Race doesn't matter
   8 = Don't know
   9 = Refused

48. Now, I want to ask you about trusting different groups of people.

48a. First, thinking about people in your immediate family, generally speaking would you say you can trust them a lot, some, a little, or not at all?

1 = A lot
2 = Some
3 = Only a little
4 = Not at all
5 = Never have contact with these people/Never been there/Not applicable
8 = Don't know
9 = Refused

48b. First, thinking about people in your neighborhood, generally speaking would you say you can trust them a lot, some, a little, or not at all?

1 = A lot
2 = Some
3 = Only a little
4 = Not at all
5 = Never have contact with these people/Never been there/Not applicable
8 = Don't know
9 = Refused

(If v26 = 1 or v27 = 2 [respondent is not employed], skip to v48e)

48c. First, thinking about your boss or supervisor, generally speaking would you say you can trust them a lot, some, a little, or not at all?

1 = A lot
2 = Some
3 = Only a little
4 = Not at all
5 = Never have contact with these people/Never been there/Not applicable
8 = Don't know
9 = Refused

48d. How about people you work with?

1 = A lot
2 = Some
3 = Only a little
4 = Not at all
5 = Never have contact with these people/Never been there/Not applicable
8 = Don't know
9 = Refused

48e. First, thinking about people at your church or place of worship, generally speaking would you say you can trust them a lot, some, a little, or not at all?

1 = A lot
2 = Some
3 = Only a little
4 = Not at all
5 = Never have contact with these people/Never been there/Not applicable
8 = Don't know
9 = Refused

48f. First, thinking about people in the same clubs or activities as you, generally speaking would you say you can trust them a lot, some, a little, or not at all?

1 = A lot
2 = Some
3 = Only a little
4 = Not at all
5 = Never have contact with these people/Never been there/Not applicable
8 = Don't know
9 = Refused

48g. First, thinking about people who work in the stores where you shop, generally speaking would you say you can trust them a lot, some, a little, or not at all?

1 = A lot
2 = Some
3 = Only a little
4 = Not at all
5 = Never have contact with these people/Never been there/Not applicable
8 = Don't know
9 = Refused

48h. First, thinking about people you encounter in your downtown area, generally speaking would you say you can trust them a lot, some, a little, or not at all?

1 = A lot
2 = Some
3 = Only a little
4 = Not at all
5 = Never have contact with these people/Never been there/Not applicable
8 = Don't know
9 = Refused

49. Lastly, in order to classify your responses with those of other

people I need to ask you a few demographic questions. First,
what is your age?

50. In general, do you consider yourself a Republican, Democrat,
Independent, or something else?

   1 = Republican
   2 = Democrat
   3 = Independent
   4 = No preference
   5 = Other
   8 = Don't know
   9 = Refused

500th. List of all California voter codes

   1 = American Libertarian Party
   2 = Libertarian Party
   3 = Peace and Freedom Party
   4 = Green Party
   5 = Natural Law Party
   6 = Reform Party
   7 = Other

51. Do you own or rent your home?

   1 = Own
   2 = Rent
   3 = Other arrangement/Live free with parents
   8 = Don't know
   9 = Refused

53. What is your religious preference: Protestant, Roman Catholic,
Jewish, Mormon, or another religious group?

   1 = Protestant (Baptist, Christian, Episcopal, Jehovah's Witness,
       Lutheran, Methodist, Presbyterian, etc.)
   2 = Roman Catholic
   3 = Jewish
   4 = Orthodox Church (Greek or Russian)
   5 = Mormon (include Church of Jesus Christ of Latter Day Saints)
   6 = Islam/Muslim
   7 = Other religion; please specify
   8 = No religion/Atheist
   88 = Don't know
   99 = Refused

54. What is the last grade or class that you completed in school?

   1 = None, or grade 1-8
   2 = High school incomplete (grades 9-11)
   3 = High school graduate (grade 12 or GED certificate)
   4 = Business, technical, or vocational school after high school

5 = Some college; no four-year degree
6 = College graduate (B.S., B.A., or other four-year degree)
7 = Postgraduate training or professional schooling after college
(e.g., toward a master's degree or Ph.D., law or medical school)
8 = Don't know
9 = Refused

55. With what ethnic or racial group do you identify—Caucasian, African American, Asian, Latino, Native American, or some other ethnicity?

1 = Caucasian
2 = African American
3 = Asian
4 = Latino
5 = Native American
6 = Other or mixed race
8 = Don't know
9 = Refused

56. In 1996, what was your total family income before taxes?

1 = Less than $10,000
2 = $10,000 to $19,999
3 = $20,000 to $29,999
4 = $30,000 to $39,999
5 = $40,000 to $49,999
6 = $50,000 to $74,999
7 = $75,000 to $99,999
8 = $100,000 or more
88 = Don't know
99 = Refused

57. We want to be sure we include people from all parts of your county. The last three questions are to give us a better idea of the area where you live. First, what is your zip code?

1 = Enter zip code
99999 = Refused

58. And what city or town do you live in?

1 = Enter name
9 = Refused

numphone. How many telephone lines do you have in your house that are for adult use?

Number

60. Gender

1 = Male
2 = Female

Parks Capacity Index Components and Intercorrelations

	V23	V25	V30D	V30E	V30M	V33C	V37_2	Participation
Will pay taxes for open space (V23)	1.000							
Will vote for bond (V25)	0.685	1.000						
Volunteered for cleanup (V30D)	0.219	-0.49	1.000					
Volunteered for environmental organization (V30E)	0.427	0.13	0.519	1.000				
Volunteered for community work (V30M)	0.385	0.135	0.656	0.485	1.000			
Contributed to specific cause (V33C)	0.621	0.392	0.092	0.381	0.348	1.000		
Favors more regulation on development (V37_2)	0.594	0.506	0.431	0.479	0.504	0.547	1.000	
Participation	0.590	0.541	0.144	0.082	0.229	0.455	0.475	1.000

NOTES: All variables are county-level averages; N = 30 counties or regions.
V23: Willing to pay local property taxes for open space.
V25: Likely to vote for an upcoming statewide park bond.
V30D: Has volunteered for adopt-a-creek, -beach, -park, or -highway group.
V30E: Has volunteered for an environmental organization.
V30M: Has volunteered for one-time or ad hoc community work.
V33C: Has joined, or contributed money to, an organization for a specific cause.
V37_2: Agrees that more should be done to regulate private development in respondent's area.
Participation: Has participated in any or all of the following face-to-face activities: adult education, self-help group, exercise class, organized religion, recreational league, card or board games with friends, e-mail or chat group, and playgroup for children.

Statewide Environmental Ballot Measures, 1924–2000

Election and year	Proposition number and type	Funding level[a]	Statewide approval rate (%)	Stated purpose(s) of the act
General 1924	11, IS	N/A	60.7	Creation of Klamath Fish and Game District
General 1928	4, LCA	6	73.7	Land acquisition, state parks
Primary 1962	5, LBA	150	47.3	Land acquisition, recreation
General 1964	1, LBA	150	62.4	Land acquisition, recreation, state parks
General 1966	3, LCA	N/A	55.5	Authorizes legislature to define, and establish assessment bases of, open space lands
General 1970	1, LBA	N/A	75.4	Clean water bond
General 1970	20, LBA	N/A	56.7	Recreation, and fish and wildlife enhancement bond
Primary 1972	9, IS	N/A	35.3	General environmental protection, reformulated fuels, pesticide controls, air emissions restrictions
General 1972	3, LCA	N/A	60.0	Environment pollution bond authorization
General 1972	8, LCA	N/A	27.1	Tax exemption for antipollution facilities
General 1972	20, IS	N/A	55.2	Coastal zone conservation
Primary 1974	1, LBA	250	59.9	Land acquisition, recreation, beaches, parks

Election and year	Proposition number and type	Funding level[a]	Statewide approval rate (%)	Stated purpose(s) of the act
Primary 1974	2, LBA	N/A	70.5	Clean water bond
General 1974	17, IS	N/A	47.1	Wild and scenic river designation for the Stanislaus River
Primary 1976	15, IS	N/A	32.5	Limits on nuclear power generation
General 1976	2, LBA	280	51.5	Land acquisition, recreation, and wildlife conservation (~5% of funds)
General 1976	3, LBA	25	41.4	Residential energy conservation bond
General 1976	12, LCA	N/A	49.0	Loans by state for energy conservation improvements in residential structures
Primary 1978	2, LBA	375	53.5	Clean water and water conservation bond
Primary 1978	3, LCA	N/A	45.2	Tax exemption for alternative energy improvements
General 1978	3, LCA	N/A	55.1	Allows the state to sell surplus coastal property to state recreation and wildlife management agencies
Primary 1980	1, LBA	495	47.0	Land acquisition, recreation, and wildlife conservation
Primary 1980	8, LCA	N/A	50.2	Alternative energy facilities source financing
General 1980	1, LBA	285	51.7	Land acquisition, recreation
General 1980	2, LBA	85	48.8	Land acquisition in Lake Tahoe region for recreation and habitat protection
General 1980	7, LCA	N/A	65.5	Tax incentives for solar energy systems
General 1980	8, LCA	N/A	53.3	Water bond, peripheral canal (pro-environment vote is "no")
General 1980	9, LBA	30	64.4	Clean water bond
Primary 1982	9, R	N/A	37.3	Peripheral canal (pro-environment vote is "no")
General 1982	4, LBA	85	52.9	Land acquisition in Lake Tahoe region, for recreation and habitat protection
General 1982	11, IS	N/A	44.1	Beverage containers
General 1982	13, IS	N/A	35.2	Water resources
Primary 1984	18, LBA	370	63.2	Land acquisition, recreation, wildlife protection

Election and year	Proposition number and type	Funding level[a]	Statewide approval rate (%)	Stated purpose(s) of the act
Primary 1984	19, LBA	85	64.0	Fish and wildlife habitat acquisition
General 1984	25, LBA	325	72.9	Clean water bond
General 1984	27, LBA	100	72.0	Hazardous substance cleanup bond
General 1984	28, LBA	75	73.5	Safe drinking water bond
Primary 1986	43, LBA	100	67.3	Grants to local park agencies
Primary 1986	44, LBA	150	74.1	Water conservation and water quality bond
General 1986	55, LBA	100	78.7	Safe drinking water bond
General 1986	65, IS	N/A	62.6	Restricts toxic discharge into drinking water; requires notice of exposure to toxics
Primary 1988	70, IBA	776	65.1	Wildlife, coastal, and parkland conservation
General 1988	82, LBA	60	62.4	Water conservation bond
General 1988	83, LBA	65	64.4	Clean water and water reclamation bond
Primary 1990	108, LBA	1,000	56.3	Passenger rail and clean air bond
Primary 1990	116, IBA	1,990	53.3	Rail transportation bond
Primary 1990	117, IS	30 in fund transfers	52.4	Wildlife and habitat protection
General 1990	125, LCA	N/A	45.6	Motor vehicle fuels tax; rail transit funding
General 1990	128, IS	300	35.7	Omnibus environmental bond measure ("Big Green")
General 1990	130, IS	742	47.9	Forestland acquisition bond, timber harvest practices regulation ("Forests Forever")
General 1990	132, ICA	N/A	55.8	Marine resources protection
General 1990	135, IS	N/A	30.4	Pesticide regulation ("Big Brown"—countermeasure to Proposition 128); pro-environment vote is "no"
General 1990	138, IS	300	28.8	Forestry program, timber harvesting practices ("Big Stump"—countermeasure to Proposition 130); pro-environment vote is "no"
General 1990	141, LIA	N/A	48.5	Applies toxics notification requirements of Proposition 65 to public agencies

Election and year	Proposition number and type	Funding level[a]	Statewide approval rate (%)	Stated purpose(s) of the act
General 1990	149, LBA	437	47.1	Land acquisition, recreation
General 1992	156, LBA	1,000	48.1	Passenger rail transit programs and bond
Primary 1994	178, LCA	N/A	45.0	Property tax exclusions for water conservation equipment
Primary 1994	180, IS	2,000	43.4	Land acquisition, recreation, and wildlife conservation
General 1994	181, LBA	1,000	34.9	Passenger rail and clean air bond
General 1994	185, IS	N/A	19.5	Public transportation trust fund, gas tax
Primary 1996	197, LIA	N/A	41.9	Repeals mountain lions' status as specially protected mammal; allows hunting; pro-environment vote is "no"
General 1996	204, LBA	995	62.8	SF–Bay Delta restoration bond, safe drinking water bond, and water quality bond
General 1998	4, IS	N/A	57.5	Prohibits trapping and poisoning of fur-bearing animals
General 1998	7, IS	228	43.6	Provides tax credits to firms developing or implementing air emissions reduction technologies
Primary 2000	12, LBA	2,100	63.2	Parkland acquisition and maintenance
Primary 2000	13, LBA	1,970	64.8	Water quality protection, watershed protection, water conservation

NOTES: An initiative bond amendment (IBA) is put on the ballot by obtaining a number of signatures from registered voters that is equal to or greater than 5 percent of the ballots cast for governor in the last election.

An initiative constitutional amendment (ICA) is put on the ballot by obtaining a number of signatures from registered voters that is equal to or greater than 8 percent of the ballots cast for governor in the last election.

An initiative statute (IS) is put on the ballot by obtaining a number of signatures from registered voters that is equal to or greater than 5 percent of the ballots cast for governor in the last election.

A legislative bond act (LBA) is proposed to the voters by a two-thirds majority vote in each house.

A legislative constitutional amendment (LCA) is proposed to the voters by a two-thirds majority vote in each house.

A legislative initiative amendment (LIA) is proposed by a two-thirds majority vote in each house to amend a statute established by initiative.

A referendum (R) is put on the ballot by obtaining a number of signatures from registered voters that is equal to or greater than 5 percent of the ballots cast for governor in the last election. A referendum is used to delete all or part of a statute passed by the legislature but not yet effective. Signatures must be gathered and certified within ninety days of the enactment of the statute.

[a] Unadjusted dollars, in millions.

Government Effectiveness Measures

	Youth programs	Park upkeep	Park number	Government is ineffective
Youth programs	1.000			
Park upkeep	0.677	1.000		
Park number	0.562	0.748	1.000	
Government is ineffective	0.471	0.297	0.448	1.000

NOTES: All variables are county-level averages; N = 30 counties or regions.
 The categories "Youth programs" (V9H), "Park upkeep" (V9K), and "Park number" (V9L) are based on the survey question "Please rate the following government services in the place where you live."
 The category "Government is ineffective" is based on summed scores on the following replies given to the question "Why would you oppose additional or new property taxes for open space?" Scores from answers to the following questions were used:
 1. "More money for government to waste" (V24a3)
 2. "Money will be mismanaged" (V24a4)
 3. "No confidence in elected board or officials" (V24a8)
 In assembling the "Government Effectiveness" index, I subtracted the "Government is ineffective" score (composed of replies to variables 24a3, 24a4, and 24a8) from the sum of "youth programs," "park upkeep," and "park number."

Environmental Awareness Index Components and Intercorrelations

	Open space publicity	Land trust awareness	Importance of open space	Taxes are important for open space (V24@1)
Open space publicity	1.000			
Land trust awareness	0.796	1.000		
Importance of open space	0.774	0.612	1.000	
Taxes are important for open space	0.355	0.505	0.355	1.000

NOTES: All variables are county-level averages; $N = 30$ counties or regions.

The category "Open space publicity" in the survey is based on affirmative responses to the survey question "Are you aware of any activity or publicity in your community regarding the acquisition, development, or maintenance of open space or parklands?" (V20).

The category "Land trust awareness" is based on affirmative responses to the survey question "Are you familiar with land trusts (nonprofit organizations that purchase land to preserve it)?" (V21).

The category "Importance of open space" is based on the response "Very important" to the survey question "How important are parks that maintain open space, with hiking trails, nature preserves, or campgrounds?" (V16).

The category "Taxes are important for open space" is based on the response "It's important to have open space" given as a reason for willingness to pay more property taxes for local land acquisition (V24@1).

Notes

1. INTRODUCTION

1. The top ten most congested metropolitan areas in the United States in 1996 were Los Angeles; Washington, D.C.; Chicago; Miami; San Francisco; Seattle; Atlanta; Detroit; San Diego; and San Bernardino–Riverside (California) (US DOT, 2001b).

2. My research assistants and I sent out two waves of mail surveys, one to county planning departments, the other to local parks and recreation agencies (see appendix 2 for the survey itself). We followed up with hundreds of telephone calls and thus obtained results for all but a handful of very small jurisdictions.

3. By way of comparison, only two other states have more acreage in federal ownership (Alaska and Nevada); only seven other states have a greater percentage of their land in federal ownership.

4. The nine Bay Area counties are Alameda, Contra Costa, Marin, Napa, San Francisco, San Mateo, Santa Clara, Solano, and Sonoma.

5. In the environmental context, outcomes refer to observable physical, behavioral, and biological indicators. As noted by Daniel J. Fiorino (1995, p. 215), these include, but are not limited to

   1. measures of activity of agencies or other actors: number of permits issued, number of inspections completed, number and types of control devices installed;
   2. measures of emissions or discharges into the air or water;
   3. ambient levels of some pollutants (ozone in air, heavy metals in water);
   4. measures of human and/or wildlife exposure to contaminants;
   5. direct measures of human health-ecosystem integrity: blood lead levels, lake acidity, species diversity.

6. As such, it is similar to the concept of "capacity for environmental policy and management" developed by Martin Jänicke. In Jänicke's model, governmental and nongovernmental actors of varying competence and strengths promote envi-

ronmental protection activities within three different frameworks: the "cognitive-informational," the "political-institutional," and the "economic-technological." "Cognitive-informational" refers to knowledge and interpretation of problems. "Political-institutional" refers to the institutions, rules, and norms governing environmental policy. "Economic-technological" refers to a nation's economic and technological resources (1997, p. 8, 12).

7. Proposition 13, implemented in 1978, was a constitutional amendment passed by initiative. According to William Fulton, "Proposition 13 rolled back property tax assessments to 1975 levels, permitted an annual increase in assessment of only 2 percent except in the event of a sale, and, for all practical purposes, capped property-tax rates at 1 percent per year. [A higher rate requires a two-thirds vote, which is very difficult to obtain.] Since property tax rates at the time were approaching 2 percent in many parts of the state, Proposition 13 cut local government revenues dramatically" (1991, p. 209). On U.S. Supreme Court takings cases, see Lucas v. South Carolina Coastal Council, 505 U.S. 1003 (1992); Dolan v. City of Tigard, 512 U.S. 374 (1994).

8. Institutions here include administrative agencies, elected policy makers, and voluntary civic associations.

2. A STATEWIDE HISTORY OF LOCAL PRESERVATION EFFORTS

1. California Government Code, sec. 65560.

2. These elements became quite elaborate; for example, in the state Parks and Recreation Information System reports of the 1960s and 1970s, which constituted early attempts at distributing—via geographic information systems (GIS)—recreation resources of different types within different distance radii. With the advent of computer-based GIS, open space resource analysts have added biological and economic (e.g., land value) targets to their overlays.

3. For example, in 1972 the state Department of Parks and Recreation spent about $2 million on local assistance grants. The federal government spent over $8 million on HUD grants in its program for undeveloped open space lands, and another $4.5 million on LWCF grants. Land acquisition expenditures by all of California's special parks and recreation districts in 1972 totaled a little over $7.8 million.

4. Uncited quotations are from my interview respondents.

5. For details on trends in local government finance since Proposition 13, see also Sheffrin and Dresch 1995; Dresch and Sheffrin 1997; Paik 1995; and O'Sullivan, Sexton, and Sheffrin 1995.

6. The state's constitution has required a two-thirds majority for approving local bond measures since the late nineteenth century. Of the measures receiving better than 50 percent approval, some two dozen were tax measures that would have gone into effect prior to Proposition 13, raising millions of dollars for local land preservation. Considering just the local park-bond measures proposed in this period, local governments requested $1.8 billion, received majority approval for $1.4 billion, but were authorized to float bonds for only about $370 million. In terms of land acquisitions, local governments could have acquired about 140,000 acres (at $10,000 per acre, a rough average in the exurban zone).

7. Of course, a handful of land trusts have been performing these roles for decades. For example, the Save-the-Redwoods League, founded in 1918, often matched state, local, or private funds for acquisition, as did the Sempervirens Fund, founded in 1900.

8. The Land Trust Alliance defines a land trust as "a local, state, or regional nonprofit organization that directly protects land for its natural, recreational, scenic, or productive value."

9. Not all land trusts reported how many acres they had protected or their annual budgets. Thus, the actual, current figures are likely to be higher. Note also that the figures on acreage do not indicate that all lands conserved by land trusts are protected by fee simple acquisition. Many of these acreages are protected through conservation easements or other nonacquisition means.

10. The margin of error for this question was ±1.5 percent.

11. In a related effort, voters soundly defeated (58 percent against) Proposition 197 in 1996, a measure that would have permitted hunting of the state's mountain lions.

3. PHYSICAL, FISCAL, AND ADMINISTRATIVE LANDSCAPES

1. California Public Resources Code, sec. 35152.

2. See Frank and Downing 1988. The figure represents 1981 dollars. The average would be about $1,510 in 2002 dollars.

3. And special recreation and parks districts spent approximately $30 million on land acquisition in 1993 (State of California Controller's Office, *Financial Transactions Concerning Special Districts, 1993–94,* [Sacramento, 1994]).

4. Even Silicon Valley engineers concern themselves with habitat degradation in their backyard. The Salmon and Steelhead Restoration Group, which goes by the name Silichip Chinook, has been effective at pushing for restoration of the salmon population in the Guadalupe River, which runs right through the heart of Silicon Valley.

5. United States Geological Survey 2000. The scale for hydrographic data is 1:100,000.

6. Ibid. The scale for elevation data is 1:250,000.

7. This GIS file consisted of many thousands of elevation measurements for each county. By taking the standard deviation of each county's elevation points, I was able to quantify whether a county was relatively hilly or flat.

8. Geographic information systems permit users to computerize maps and to overlay many different sorts of spatial data—such as the location of park parcels, roads, and creeks—with demographic, biological, and physical data. These systems allow users to rapidly and easily view spatial patterns of such data without redrawing paper maps.

4. CIVIC AND ENVIRONMENTAL VOLUNTARISM

1. Appendixes 3, 5, and 6 provide the index components and intercorrelations used to construct these models.

2. Rice and Sumberg 1997. The two researchers measured civic culture in

terms of civic engagement, political equality, solidarity, trust and tolerance, and social structures of cooperation (membership in professional societies, clubs, church groups). They measured government performance as policy liberalism and innovation, and administrative effectiveness.

3. Appendix 4 lists all environmental measures that appeared on state ballots from 1924 to 2000.

5. POLICY ENTREPRENEURSHIP

1. The taxpayers' association argued in court that, because the agency would levy property taxes, the advisory vote needed a two-thirds majority under Proposition 13, substantially more than the 57 percent that it received.

2. In its application for state funds, the Marin County Open Space District pointed out that almost 60 percent of Marin City's residents were African American, many of whom earned very low incomes. The city's public housing residents earned $9,300 per year in average income for the late 1990s, far below the county's average, which was well above $30,000 per year for all of that decade (MCOSD 1999).

3. From personal communication regarding Rose, concerning H.R. 3632, a bill to revise the boundaries of the Golden Gate National Recreation Area (Miska 2000).

6. POLICY CAPACITY ACROSS THE LANDSCAPE

1. The matter of increases in government spending was covered by question number 36: "The next question is about government services and spending in general. Which do you think would be best: for government to reduce spending and provide fewer services, to continue the services it now provides even if that means no reduction in spending, or to provide more services even if that means increased spending?" Figure 27 uses the percentage of respondents answering, "Provide more services even if it means an increase in spending." The matter of greater regulation of private development was covered by question number 37: "What do you think is most important in your area: to promote private development even if it means loss of some open space, or regulate development to protect open space, or do you think the balance between regulation and development is about right in your area?" Figure 27 uses the percentage of respondents answering "Regulate private development."

2. The question they responded to: "If an election were held today, would you vote yes or no on a local initiative that would slow down the pace of development in your city or community, even if this meant having less economic growth?"

3. The list of fastest growing counties comes from the U.S. Census Bureau (2001).

4. The opinion research firm Fairbank, Maslin, Maullin and Associates polled likely voters around the state in January 2000, prior to the March 2000 primary, and found that 62 percent of Latino respondents said they were definitely or probably going to vote for Proposition 12. White respondents sup-

ported the measure at the rate of 52 percent. The survey was commissioned by the Nature Conservancy of California.

5. In the first instance, N (the sample size) was 3,919, with a margin of error of ±1.6 percent. Twenty-five percent of whites rated the number of parks as fair or poor (N = 2,704, margin of error = ±1.9 percent); 65 percent rated open space as very important (N = 2,835, margin of error = ±1.8 percent). In the second instance, N was 440, with a margin of error of ±4 percent.

6. The N for all respondents was 4,100, with a margin of error of ±1.5 percent; for Latinos it was 440, with a margin of error of ±4 percent.

7. Interestingly, a few development corporations made generous donations to the Propositions 12 and 13 campaigns, totaling about $400,000. As an Orange County planner remarked, "The big landowners . . . realize that parks are very good for business. The more parks you have, the more houses you sell; it's that simple."

8. The supermajority states are Arizona, Arkansas, California, Colorado, Delaware, Florida, Louisiana, Mississippi, Missouri, Nevada, Oklahoma, Oregon, South Dakota, and Washington (Poulson 2001).

9. See also the Planning and Conservation League's policy reform recommendations for land use (http://www.pcl.org).

References

Agnew, John A. 1987. *Place and Politics: The Geographical Mediation of State and Society.* Boston: Allen and Unwin.

Air Resources Board (ARB). 1998. *California Ambient Air Quality Data, 1980–1997.* Sacramento, December.

Alameda County. 1956. *The Recreation Plan: A Plan for Beaches, Parks, and Recreation Areas, Being a Part of the Master Plan.* Oakland, Calif.: Alameda County Planning Commission.

Almond, Gabriel A. 1997. Foreword to *Culture Matters: Essays in Honor of Aaron Wildavsky,* ed. Richard J. Ellis and Michael Thompson. Boulder, Colo.: Westview Press.

Andrews, Richard N. L. 1999. *Managing the Environment, Managing Ourselves: A History of American Environmental Policy.* New Haven, Conn.: Yale University Press.

Arax, Mark. 1995. "Trouble in California's Heartland." *Los Angeles Times,* December 6.

Bank of America. 1996. *Beyond Sprawl: New Patterns of Growth to Fit the New California.* San Francisco: BankAmerica Corporation.

Barrett, Thomas S., and Putnam Livermore. 1983. *The Conservation Easement in California.* Covelo, Calif.: Island Press.

Benfield, F. Kaid, Matthew D. Raimi, and Donald D. T. Chen. 1999. *Once There Were Greenfields: How Urban Sprawl Is Undermining America's Environment, Economy, and Social Fabric.* Washington, D.C.: Natural Resources Defense Council.

Berry, Jeffrey M., Kent E. Portney, and Ken Thomson. 1993. *The Rebirth of Urban Democracy.* Washington, D.C.: Brookings Institution.

Borenstein, Seth. 2000. "House OKs Billions for Open Space." *San Jose Mercury News,* May 12, pp. A1, A21.

Borenstein, Seth, and Paul Rogers. 1999. "Clinton Boosts Open Space." *San Jose Mercury News,* January 12.

Bowler, Shaun, and Todd Donovan. 1994. "Economic Conditions and Voting on Ballot Propositions." *American Politics Quarterly* 22:27–40.

Bowman, Ann O'M., and Richard Kearney. 1988. "Dimensions of State Government Capability." *Western Political Quarterly* 41:341–62.

Boyne, George A. 1992. "Local Government Structure and Performance: Lessons from America?" *Public Administration* 70:333–57.

———. 1985. "Review Article: Theory, Methodology, and Results in Political Science: The Case of Output Studies." *British Journal of Political Science* 15:473–515.

Brace, Paul, and Aubrey Jewett. 1995. "Field Essay: The State of State Politics Research." *Political Research Quarterly* 48:643–81.

Burby, Raymond J., and Peter J. May. 1997. *Making Governments Plan: State Experiments in Managing Land Use.* Baltimore, Md.: Johns Hopkins University Press.

California Department of Conservation. Farmland Mapping and Monitoring Project, 1984–1998. Http://www.consrv.ca.gov/dlrp/FMMP/index_fmmp.htm.

California Department of Finance. 1998, 1999. *California Statistical Abstract.* Sacramento.

California Department of Parks and Recreation (Cal DPR). 1994. *California Outdoor Recreation Plan, 1993.* Sacramento: State of California Resources Agency.

———. 1993. *California Outdoor Recreation Plan.* Sacramento: State of California Resources Agency.

———. 1988. *Local Parks and Recreation Agencies in California: A 1987 Survey.* Sacramento: State of California Resources Agency.

———. 1982. *Recreation in California: Issues and Actions: 1981–1985.* Sacramento: State of California Resources Agency.

California Fair Political Practices Commission. 1988. *1988 Primary Election Campaign Receipts and Expenditures, January 1, 1987 through June 30, 1988.* Sacramento.

California Governor's Office. 1996. *California State Budget.* Sacramento: Governor's Office.

California Governor's Office of Planning and Research. 2001. California Planners' Information Network. Http://calpin.ca.gov.

———. 1995–1999. *The California Planners' Book of Lists.* Sacramento: Governor's Office of Research. Http://ceres.ca.gov/planning/bol/1999.

California Legislature. Joint Committee on Open Space Land. 1969. *Preliminary Report.* Sacramento, March.

California Secretary of State. 2000. *Statement of Votes, 1924–2000.* Sacramento. Http://www.ss.ca.gov.

California State Board of Equalization. 1995–2000. *Local Agency Formation Commission Rolls.* Sacramento.

Center for California Studies. 1994–1997. *California County, City, and School District Election Outcomes.* Sacramento: California State University, Sacramento.

Colangelo, Jim. 2000. Assistant County Administrative Officer, Environmental Resource Policy Division, Monterey County. Personal communications, June 20.

Coleman, James S. 1988. "Social Capital in the Creation of Human Capital." *American Journal of Sociology* 4, suppl., pp. S95–S120.

Dana, Samuel T., and Myron Krueger. 1958. *California Lands: Ownership, Use, and Management*. Washington, D.C.: American Forestry Association.

Dasmann, Raymond. 1965. *The Destruction of California*. New York: Macmillan.

David and Lucile Packard Foundation. 2000. "Conservation Program." Http://www.packfound.org.

Derr, Chris. 1997. "Folsom Council Orders Revisions to Sphere of Influence Proposal." *Sacramento Bee,* July 27, p. N1.

Diringer, Elliot. 1985. "Growth Vote Sends Message to Politicians." *San Francisco Chronicle,* November 7, p. 1.

Dresch, Marla, and Steven M. Sheffrin. 1997. *Who Pays for Development Fees and Exactions?* San Francisco: Public Policy Institute of California, June.

Edwards, Bob, and Michael W. Foley. 1998. "Civil Society and Social Capital beyond Putnam." *American Behavioral Scientist* 42, no. 1 (September): 124–39.

Egan, Timothy. 1998. "The New Politics of Urban Sprawl." *New York Times,* November 15, p. WK1 (L).

———. 1996. "Urban Sprawl Strains Western States." *New York Times,* December 29, pp. 1N, 1L.

Field, Christopher B., Gretchen C. Daily, Frank W. Davis, Steven Gaines, Pamela A. Matson, John Melack, and Norman L. Miller. 1999. *Confronting Climate Change in California: Ecological Impacts on the Golden State.* Cambridge, Mass.: Union of Concerned Scientists and Ecological Society of America. Http://www.ucsusa.org.

Fiorino, Daniel J. 1995. *Making Environmental Policy.* Berkeley and Los Angeles: University of California Press.

Folz, David H., and Joseph M. Hazlett. 1991. "Public Participation and Recycling Performance: Explaining Program Success." *Public Administration Review* 51:526–32.

Frank, James E., and Paul B. Downing. 1988. "Patterns of Impact Fees." In *Development Impact Fees: Policy Rationale, Theory, and Issues,* ed. Arthur C. Nelson. Chicago: Planners Press.

Fulton, William. 1997. *The Reluctant Metropolis: The Politics of Urban Growth in Los Angeles.* Point Arena, Calif.: Solano Press.

———. 1991. *Guide to California Planning.* Point Arena, Calif.: Solano Press.

Glickfeld, Madelyn, Sonia Jacques, Walter Kieser, and Todd Olson. 1995. "Implementation Techniques and Strategies for Conservation Plans." *Land Use and Environment Forum* (winter): 12–27.

Granato, Jim, Ronald Inglehart, and David Leblang. 1996. "Cultural Values and Economic Development." *American Journal of Political Science* 40, no. 3 (August).

Green, Morgan. 2000. "Group Seeks to Curb Urban Sprawl: Initiative: Local

Agency Would Issue Bonds to Purchase Undeveloped Lands." *Santa Barbara News Press,* June 21.

Greenbelt Alliance. 2000. Http://www.greenbelt.org.

———. 1992. *The Bay Area's Public Lands: Findings from the 1992 Survey.* San Francisco: Greenbelt Alliance.

GreenInfo Network. 2000. "Information and Mapping in the Public Interest." Http://www.greeninfo.org.

Harbinger Communications. 1998. *The Harbinger File: A Directory of Citizen Groups, Government Agencies, and Environmental Education Programs Concerned with California Issues.* Santa Cruz, Calif.: Harbinger Communications.

Hise, Greg, and William Deverell. 2000. *Eden by Design: The 1930 Olmsted-Bartholomew Plan for the Los Angeles Region.* Berkeley and Los Angeles: University of California Press.

Hodgkinson, Virginia A., Heather A. Gorski, Stephen M. Noga, and E. B. Knauft. 1995. *Giving and Volunteering in the United States, 1994.* Vol. 2. Washington, D.C.: Independent Sector.

Inglehart, Ronald. 1988. "The Renaissance of Political Culture." *American Political Science Review* 82, no. 4 (December).

Ito, Donald H. 1977. *Recreation Technical and Information Paper 9: Recreational Acreage and Acres Per 1,000 Population for Cities, Counties, and Special Districts.* Sacramento: State of California Resources Agency.

Jänicke, Martin. 1997. "The Political System's Capacity for Environmental Policy." In *National Environmental Policies: A Comparative Study of Capacity-Building,* ed. Martin Jänicke and Helmut Weidner. New York: Springer.

Janofsky, Michael. 1999. "Gore Offers Plan to Control Suburban Sprawl." *New York Times,* January 12, p. A16.

Jensen, Deborah, Margaret Torn, and John Harte. 1993. *In Our Own Hands: A Strategy for Conserving Biological Diversity in California.* Berkeley and Los Angeles: University of California Press.

John, Dewitt. 1994. *Civic Environmentalism: Alternatives to Regulation in States and Communities.* Washington, D.C.: CQ Press.

Kaplan, Marshall, Toddi Steelman, and Allan Wallis. 1999. *Sprawl and Growth Management: Problems, Experience, and Opportunity.* Denver: Institute for Policy Research and Implementation.

Kasler, Dale. 1998. "Farms and Suburbs Can Make Troublesome Neighbors." *Sacramento Bee,* October 19, pp. A1, A10.

Kettl, Donald F., and H. Brinton Milward, eds. 1996. *The State of Public Management.* Baltimore, Md.: Johns Hopkins University Press.

Kingdon, John W. 1995. *Agendas, Alternatives, and Public Policies.* 2d ed. New York: HarperCollins College Publishers.

Kline, Jeffrey, and Dennis Wichelns. 1998. "Measuring Heterogeneous Preferences for Preserving Farmland and Open Space." *Ecological Economics* 26:211–24.

Koehler, Dave. 2000. Executive Director, San Joaquin River Parkway and Conservation Trust. Personal communication, January 21.

Ladd, Helen F. 1998. *Local Government Tax and Land Use Policies in the*

United States: Understanding the Links. Northampton, Mass.: Edward Elgar Publishing.

Landis, John D. 1992. "Do Growth Controls Work? A New Assessment." *Journal of the American Planning Association* 58, no. 4 (autumn): 489–508.

Land Trust Alliance. 2001. "More Than $7.4 Billion Committed to Open Space Protection." January 18. Http://www.lta.org/publicpolicy/referenda2000.htm.

———. 1998. *1997 National Directory of Conservation Land Trusts.* Washington, D.C.: Land Trust Alliance.

———. 1995. *1995 National Directory of Conservation Land Trusts.* Washington, D.C.: Land Trust Alliance.

Land Trust Exchange. 1985. *1985–86 National Directory of Local and Regional Land Conservation Organizations.* Bar Harbor, Maine: Land Trust Exchange.

Leo, Christopher, Mary Ann Beavis, Andrew Carver, and Robyne Turner. 1998. "Is Urban Sprawl Back on the Political Agenda? Local Growth Control, Regional Growth Management, and Politics." *Urban Affairs Review* 34, no. 2 (November): 179–212.

Lester, James P., and Emmett N. Lombard. 1990. "The Comparative Analysis of State Environmental Policy." *Natural Resources Journal* 30:301–19.

Levi, Margaret. 1996. "Social and Unsocial Capital: A Review Essay of Robert Putnam's *Making Democracy Work.*" *Politics and Society* 24, no. 1 (March): 45–55.

Los Angeles County. 1948. *Report on Master Plan of Parks.* Los Angeles: Regional Planning Commission.

Luten, Daniel B. 1984. Foreword to the 1984 reprint of the *Olmsted-Hall Report,* in *Report on Proposed Park Reservations for East Bay Cities, California.* Prepared for the Bureau of Public Administration. Berkeley and Los Angeles: University of California.

Marin County. 1943. *Master Recreation Plan.* San Rafael, Calif.: Marin County Planning Commission.

Marin County Open Space District. 1999. *MCOSD Application for Funds from the Bay Area Conservancy Program, State Coastal Conservancy, for Use toward the Acquisition of the 94-Acre Keig Property in Southern Marin County.* September 3. Marin, Calif.: MCOSD.

Martin, David. 1998. Grants Database Manager, California State Department of Parks and Recreation. Personal communication.

McCulloch, Frank. 1989. "'Perestroika' in the Bay Area." *San Francisco Chronicle,* December 17.

Meral, Gerald. 2001. Director, Planning and Conservation League, personal communication.

Midpeninsula Regional Open Space District (MROSD). 1995. *Purchase of 907-Acre Jacques Ridge Is Complete.* Press release, January 13.

Miller, Christian. 1998. "A Growth Plan Run Amok." *Los Angeles Times,* December 27.

Mintrom, Michael. 2000. *Policy Entrepreneurs and School Choice.* Washington, D.C.: Georgetown University Press.

Miska, Ron. 2000. Planner, Marin County Open Space District, personal communication.

Molotch, Harvey. 1976. "The City as Growth Machine." *American Journal of Sociology* 82:309–32.

Monterey County. 1944. *Park and Recreation Plan*. Monterey, Calif.: Monterey County Planning Commission.

Myers, Phyllis. 1999. *Livability at the Ballot Box: State and Local Referenda on Parks, Conservation, and Smarter Growth, Election Day 1998*. Washington, D.C.: Brookings Institution, January.

Nelson, Arthur C. 1999. "Comparing States with and without Growth Management: Analysis Based on Indicators with Policy Implications." *Land Use Policy* 16:121–27.

———, ed. 1988. *Development Impact Fees: Policy Rationale, Theory, and Issues*. Chicago: Planners Press.

Nivola, Pietro S. 1999. "Make Way for Sprawl." *Washington Post*, June 1, p. A15.

Nolte, Carl. 1999. "Sprawl, Clutter Define Fresno: Civic Corruption Has Splotched the City's Image." *San Francisco Chronicle*, September 1.

Olmsted Brothers and Bartholomew and Associates, Consultants. 1930. *Parks, Playgrounds, and Beaches for the Los Angeles Region: A Report Submitted to the Citizens' Committee on Parks, Playgrounds, and Beaches*. Los Angeles, n.p.

Olmsted Brothers and Ansel F. Hall. [1930] 1984. *Report on Proposed Park Reservations for East Bay Cities, California*. Prepared for the Bureau of Public Administration and the University of California. Reprint, Berkeley and Los Angeles: University of California Press.

O'Sullivan, Arthur, Terri A. Sexton, and Steven M. Sheffrin. 1995. *Property Taxes and Tax Revolts: The Legacy of Proposition 13*. New York: Cambridge University Press.

Paik, Helen C. 1995. *Local Government Finances since Proposition 13: An Historical Primer*. Sacramento: California Research Bureau of the California State Library.

Pendall, R. 1999. "Do Land-Use Controls Cause Sprawl?" *Environment and Planning B: Planning and Design* 26:555–71.

People for Open Space (POS). 1978. *Annual Report*. San Francisco: POS.

———. 1969. *The Case for Open Space in the San Francisco Bay Area*. San Francisco: POS.

Pincetl, Stephanie. 1999. *Transforming California: A Political History of Land Use and Development*. Baltimore, Md.: Johns Hopkins University Press.

Porter, Douglas R. 1987. "Slow-Growth Gusto Hits LA." *Urban Land* (December 30).

Poulson, Barry. 2001. "Fiscal Discipline Project: Super-Majority Requirements." Http://www.colorado.edu/Economics/taxpolicy/SuperMajority/supermajority .html.

Press, Daniel. 1995. "Environmental Regionalism and the Struggle for California." *Society and Natural Resources* 8, no. 4.

———. 1994. *Democratic Dilemmas in the Age of Ecology: Trees and Toxics in the American West*. Durham, N.C.: Duke University Press.

Press, Daniel, Daniel F. Doak, and Paul Steinberg. 1996. "The Role of Local Government in Rare Species Conservation." *Conservation Biology* 10, no. 6 (December).

Public Policy Institute of California (PPIC). 2000. *Special Survey on Californians and the Environment.* San Francisco: PPIC. Http://www.ppic.org.

Putnam, Robert D. 1995. "Tuning In, Tuning Out: The Strange Disappearance of Social Capital in America." *PS: Political Science and Politics* 28, no. 4 (December): 664–83.

———. 1993. *Making Democracy Work: Civic Traditions in Modern Italy.* Princeton, N.J.: Princeton University Press.

Rice, Tom W., and Alexander F. Sumberg. 1997. "Civic Culture and Government Performance in the American States." *Publius—the Journal of Federalism* 27, no. 1 (winter): 99–114.

Richter, Brian D., and Kent H. Redford. 1999. "The Art (and Science) of Brokering Deals between Conservation and Use." *Conservation Biology* 13, no. 6 (December).

Ringquist, Evan J. 1993. *Environmental Protection at the State Level: Politics and Progress in Controlling Pollution.* Armonk, N.Y.: M. E. Sharpe.

Ringquist, Evan J., J. A. Lee, and R. T. Ervin. 1995. "Evaluating the Environmental Effects of Agricultural Policy: The Soil Bank, the CRP, and Airborne Particulate Concentrations." *Policy Studies Journal* 23, no. 3.

Roberts, Nancy C., and Paula J. King. 1996. *Transforming Public Policy: Dynamics of Policy Entrepreneurship and Innovation.* San Francisco: Jossey-Bass, Publishers.

Robertson, David B., and Dennis R. Judd. 1989. *The Development of American Public Policy: The Structure of Policy Restraint.* Glenview, Ill.: Scott, Foresman, and Company.

Rochon, Thomas R. 1998. *Culture Moves: Ideas, Activism, and Changing Values.* Princeton, N.J.: Princeton University Press.

Rogers, Paul. 1996a. "Big Chunk of Big Sur Preserved." *San Jose Mercury News,* December 4, pp. A1, A18.

———. 1996b. "County Plans to Buy Big Area for Park Use." *San Jose Mercury News,* August 20, p. A1.

———. 1996c. "Park Piggy Bank Rescue Under Way." *San Jose Mercury News,* January 7, pp. 1B, 4B.

Rome, Adam W. 1998. "William Whyte, Open Space, and Environmental Activism." *Geographical Review* 88, no. 2 (April): 259–74.

Rose, Annette. 2000. "Statement of Annette Rose, Marin County Board of Supervisors, Marin County, California, Concerning H.R. 3632, a Bill to Revise the Boundaries of the Golden Gate National Recreation Area." May 16.

San Diego, City of. 1956. *A Master Plan of Parks and Recreation.* San Diego, Calif.: City Planning Commission and Park and Recreation Commission.

Sanger, Mary Bryna. 1999. Review of *Transforming Public Policy: Dynamics of Policy Entrepreneurship and Innovation,* by Nancy C. Roberts and Paula J. King. *Journal of Policy Analysis and Management* 18, no. 1:178–81.

San Jose Mercury News. 1999. "IBM Open-Space Promise Needs to Be Locked In." March 31, Op-Ed., p. 6B.

Santa Cruz, City of. 1994. *City of Santa Cruz Greenbelt Master Plan.* Santa Cruz, Calif.: City of Santa Cruz Planning and Community Development Department.

Schneider, Anne, and Helen Ingram. 1990. "Behavioral Assumptions of Policy Tools." *Journal of Politics* 52.

Schneider, Mark, Paul Teske, and Michael Mintrom. 1995. *Public Entrepreneurs: Agents for Change in American Government.* Princeton, N.J.: Princeton University Press.

Schrag, Peter. 1998. *Paradise Lost: California's Experience, America's Future.* New York: New Press.

Sharpe, L. J., and K. Newton. 1984. *Does Politics Matter? The Determinants of Public Policy.* Oxford: Clarendon Press.

Sheffrin, Steven M., and Marla Dresch. 1995. *Estimating the Tax Burden in California.* Berkeley, Calif.: California Policy Seminar.

Shen, Q. 1996. "Spatial Impacts of Locally Enacted Growth Controls: The San Francisco Bay Region in the 1980s." *Environment and Planning B: Planning and Design* 23:61–91.

Shutkin, William. 2000. *The Land That Could Be: Environmentalism and Democracy in the Twenty-First Century.* Cambridge: MIT Press.

Sierra Club. 1999. *Solving Sprawl.* Washington, D.C.: Sierra Club. Http://www.sierraclub.org/sprawl/report99/.

Skocpol, Theda, and Morris P. Fiorina. 1999. "Making Sense of the Civic Engagement Debate." In *Civic Engagement in American Democracy,* ed. Morris P. Fiorina and Theda Skocpol. Washington, D.C.: Brookings Institution.

State of California. State Controller's Office. 1969–1996. *Report on Financial Transactions Concerning Special Districts.* Sacramento.

Steinberg, Paul. 1999. "Transnational Relations and the Politics of Species Conservation in Poor Countries: Evidence from Costa Rica and Bolivia, 1967–1997." Ph.D. diss., University of California, Santa Cruz.

Stone, Deborah. 1997. *Policy Paradox: The Art of Political Decision Making.* New York: W. W. Norton.

Stonecash, Jeffrey M. 1996. "The State Politics Literature: Moving beyond Covariation Studies and Pursuing Politics." *Polity* 28, no. 4:559–79.

Szasz, Andrew. 1994. *EcoPopulism: Toxic Waste and the Movement for Environmental Justice.* Minneapolis: University of Minnesota Press.

Trust for Public Land (TPL). 1997. *Building the American Commons: Twenty-Five Years at the Trust for Public Land.* San Francisco: Trust for Public Land.

United States Census Bureau. 2002. "Census of Construction, 1997." Http://www.census.gov/prod/www/abs/cons-hou.html#contsvy.

———. 2001. "County Population Estimates." Http://www.census.gov/population/www/estimates/countypop.html.

United States Department of Agriculture (US DOA). 2002. "Census of Agriculture, 1964–1997." Http://www.nass.usda.gov/census.

United States Department of Interior (US DOI). 2001. "Lands Legacy: Lasting

Protection for America's Natural Treasures." February 22. Http://www.doi .gov/iga/ll1.htm.

United States Department of Transportation (US DOT). 2001a. "Smart Growth." February 22. Http://www.fta.dot.gov/research/polplan/susdev/smgrow/smgrow .htm.

———. 2001b. "Congestion Index and Cost Values." Bureau of Transportation Statistics. January 18. Http://www.bts.gov/ntda/nts/NTS99/data/Chapter1/ 1–56.html.

United States Environmental Protection Agency (US EPA). 2001. "Smart Growth and Communities." February 22. Http://www.epa.gov/livability/.

United States Geological Survey. 2000. *Digital Line Graph, with Subsequent Processing by the State of California Spatial Information Library.* Washington, D.C.: USGS.

United States Outdoor Recreation Resources Review Commission (USORRRC). 1962. *The Future of Outdoor Recreation in Metropolitan Regions of the United States.* Vol. 3. Washington, D.C.: Outdoor Recreation Resources Review Commission.

Urry, John. 1990. "Conclusion: Place and Politics." In *Place, Policy, and Politics: Do Localities Matter?* ed. Michael Harloe, C. G. Pickvance, and John Urry. Boston: Unwin Hyman.

Varshney, Ashutosh. 1998. "Ethnic Conflict and Civic Life." Paper prepared for the American Political Science Meeting, Boston, Mass., August 31–September 4, 1998.

Vellinga, Mary Lynne. 1999. "Pressure Builds at Urban Boundary." *Sacramento Bee,* January 17.

Verardo, Denzil. 1997. Deputy Director for Administration, California Department of Parks and Recreation. Personal communication, March 27.

Vig, Norman, and Michael Kraft, eds. 1994. *Environmental Policy in the 1990s.* 2d ed. Washington, D.C.: CQ Press.

Weaver, R. Kent, and Bert A. Rockman. 1993. "Assessing the Effects of Institutions." In *Do Institutions Matter? Government Capabilities in the United States and Abroad,* ed. R. Kent Weaver and Bert A. Rockman. Washington, D.C.: Brookings Institution.

Wildermuth, John. 1997. "Long Haul to American Dream." *San Francisco Chronicle,* March 18, pp. A1, A6.

Williams, Bruce A., and Albert R. Matheny. 1995. *Democracy, Dialogue, and Environmental Disputes: The Contested Languages of Social Regulation.* New Haven, Conn.: Yale University Press.

Wilson, Marshall. 1999. "Ready or Not, Gilroy Growing." *San Francisco Chronicle,* September 9, pp. A1, A20.

Wolverton, Troy G. R. 1998. "Milpitas to Vote on Urban Limits." *San Jose Mercury News,* October 11, pp. 1B–2B.

Wright, John B. 1994. "Designing and Applying Conservation Easements." *Journal of the American Planning Association* 60, no. 3:380–88.

———. 1993. *Rocky Mountain Divide: Selling and Saving the West.* Austin: University of Texas Press.

Yaryan, Willie. 1999. "One Hundred Years of Saving the Redwoods: The Sempervirens Club and the Sempervirens Fund." Manuscript, University of California, Santa Cruz.

Yost, Walt. 1997. "The Last Open Space: Gum Ranch Development Moves Ahead minus Shopping Center." *Sacramento Bee,* January 19, p. N1.

———. 1995. "Revised Gum Ranch Plan Cuts Homes, Adds Park." *Sacramento Bee,* January 22, p. N1.

Index

Compositor:	BookMatters, Berkeley
Text:	10/13 Sabon
Display:	Sabon
Printer and binder:	Friesens Corporation